LEADING
WOMEN

Wilma Mankiller

LIZ SONNEBORN

Marshall Cavendish
Benchmark
New York

Other Marshall Cavendish Offices:
Marshall Cavendish International (Asia) Private Limited, 1 New Industrial Road, Singapore 536196 • Marshall Cavendish International (Thailand) Co Ltd. 253 Asoke, 12th Flr, Sukhumvit 21 Road, Klongtoey Nua, Wattana, Bangkok 10110, Thailand • Marshall Cavendish (Malaysia) Sdn Bhd, Times Subang, Lot 46, Subang Hi-Tech Industrial Park, Batu Tiga, 40000 Shah Alam, Selangor Darul Ehsan, Malaysia

Marshall Cavendish is a trademark of Times Publishing Limited
All websites were available and accurate when this book was sent to press.

Library of Congress Cataloging-in-Publication Data
Sonneborn, Liz.
Wilma Mankiller / by Liz Sonneborn.
p. cm. — (Leading women)
Summary: "Presents the biography of Wilma Mankiller against the backdrop of her political, historical, and cultural environment"—Provided by publisher.
Includes bibliographical references and index.
ISBN 978-0-7614-4959-1
1. Mankiller, Wilma Pearl, 1945—Juvenile literature. 2. Cherokee women—Biography—Juvenile literature. 3. Cherokee Indians—Politics and government—Juvenile literature. I. Title.
E99.C5M338 2010
973'.049755—dc22 [B]
2009029399

Editor: Deborah Grahame   Art Director: Anahid Hamparian
Publisher: Michelle Bisson   Series Designer: Nancy Sabato
Photo research by Connie Gardner
Cover image by Aimee Vance

The photographs in this book are used by permission and through the courtesy of: *AP Photo*: 74; Jerry Willis, 1; Orlin Wagner, 64; Charles Tasnadi, 87; Dennis Cook, 93; *Getty Images*: Stephen Sugerman, 4; Ernst Haas, 16; Hulton Archive, 20, 28, Time and Life Pictures, 30, 37, 71; Panoramic Images, 42; *Corbis*: Bettmann, 85; Galen Rowell, 24; Buddy Mays, 88; *The Image Works*: George Gardner, 26; *Native Stock Photos*, 9, 13, 52.

Printed in Malaysia (T)
135642

CONTENTS

CHAPTER ONE

Mankiller Flats

O N A CHILLY MID-DECEMBER DAY IN 1985, a young woman in a crisp black suit stood before a crowd in a plush council chamber. She raised one hand and placed the other on a Bible. In a clear, calm voice, she said, "I, Wilma P. Mankiller, do solemnly swear, or affirm, that I will faithfully execute the duties of Principal Chief of the Cherokee Nation. And will, to the best of my abilities, preserve, protect, and defend the Constitutions of the Cherokee Nation and the United States of America. I swear, or affirm, further that I will do everything within my power to promote the culture, heritage, and tradition of the Cherokee Nation."

Mankiller took her place behind a nearby podium and prepared to give her first address as the leader of the Cherokee Nation of Oklahoma. The event was historic. She was the first woman to serve as principal chief of the Cherokees, who, after the Navajos, are the second-largest Indian tribe in the United States.

Mankiller thanked her supporters. She then turned her attention to the job before her. Mankiller wanted to reassure the Cherokees that her administration would not make any radical changes. She knew that some people were a bit uncomfortable with the idea of a female chief, and they were fearful of what she might do.

> **I think there's a bit of nervousness in the Cherokee Nation. . . . I think any time there's a change, people wonder what's going to happen.**

Wilma Mankiller, photographed in 2005 at an American Indian College Fund gala, where she was honored for her commitment to increasing educational opportunities for Indian children.

Mankiller's words spoke to more than the Cherokees' sense of uncertainty. They applied just as well to her own feelings about the future. The forty-year-old grandmother knew that becoming principal chief would change her life, but she had no way of anticipating how much. In the years to come, Mankiller would wrestle with an array of unforeseen challenges while leading the Cherokees in the final years of the twentieth century. At the same time, she would also become a best-selling author, a renowned scholar, a national advocate for American-Indian rights, and, most unexpectedly of all, a celebrity known around the world.

The story of Wilma Pearl Mankiller begins on November 18, 1945, when she was born in Tahlequah, the capital of the Cherokee Nation. Her family lived nearby on a tract of land known as Mankiller Flats. Located in Adair County, the plot was tucked into the foothills of the Ozark Mountains. Foxes and deer ran wild through its forests of oak, sycamore, and dogwood.

The Mankillers had lived on the plot for decades. In the late nineteenth century, it became the property of Wilma's father's father, John Mankiller. Wilma never met her grandfather, who died nine years before she was born.

Wilma's father, Charley Mankiller, was born in a small wooden house on Mankiller Flats. As a boy, he was sent to live at a boarding school for Indian children near Tahlequah. The school was run by the U.S. government. Its teachers taught the students how to speak and write in English. They also instructed them in non-Indian ways. The goal of Indian boarding schools was to make children forget about their own Indian cultures and live just like white Americans.

Charley Mankiller spent twelve years at his boarding school. He learned to speak English well because his teachers beat him if he spoke the Cherokee language. He also learned to read and came to love books. But even as he took in his teachers' lessons, Charley never forgot about Mankiller Flats. He still remembered by heart the old Cherokee stories his relatives told him when he was small.

A CHEROKEE FAMILY

When he left school, Charley returned to Mankiller Flats. There, he made his living off the land. He grew strawberries and peanuts. He also picked berries and beans to earn extra money. Each fall, Charley traveled to a farm in Colorado to work as a laborer. He helped harvest broomcorn, which was used to make brooms.

Charley began dating a young woman named Clara Sitton, who was known by her middle name, Irene. She was white, but she had lived in Adair County for a long time and had many Cherokee friends. After a quick courtship, Charley and Irene decided to get married, even though she was only fifteen. Irene's grandmother was not happy. She said Charley, at twenty-one, was way too old for Irene. She also did not like the idea of a white woman marrying a Cherokee man.

The young couple ignored her objections. Charley and Irene got married and settled down on Mankiller Flats. When Wilma was born, they had been together for eight years and already had five children. Eventually Irene would give birth to a total of eleven children. As the sixth child, Wilma was right in the middle.

GROWING UP POOR

When Wilma was young, many Americans were enjoying an economic boom. The Mankillers, however, struggled financially. Like most rural Cherokees, they had trouble getting by. But the whole family worked hard to make sure everyone had enough to eat. As Wilma later recalled,

" Somehow, we always had food on the table. "

Wilma and her sisters helped their mother grow tomatoes, beans, and corn. The children also trampled through the woods on the lookout for wild onions, mushrooms, and berries. Her father and brothers hunted and fished. Charley and Wilma's oldest brother Don might come home with a groundhog or a wild pig. The smaller boys might catch frogs or squirrels. In her autobiography, Mankiller remembers how her mother breaded and fried squirrel meat and served it with gravy made from the drippings.

The Mankiller home was modest. Built by Charley, it only had four rooms. The walls and floors were covered with bare planks of wood. The roof was made of tin.

In the winter, the Mankillers relied on a wood stove for heat. Without electricity, they lit coal-oil lamps when the sun went down. The small house also lacked running water. They had to carry water for washing and cooking from a spring about a quarter mile away.

The Mankillers and their Cherokee neighbors never had much money, but they had a rich social life. Often, they got together for community events and tribal ceremonies. Wilma particularly liked ceremonial dances. Held outside, the events sometimes lasted all day

Like the Mankillers, many Cherokee families throughout history have made their living off the land. This reconstructed Cherokee community in Tahlequah, Oklahoma, shows what a Cherokee homestead looked like in the 1800s.

and night. Children ran around, played, and feasted on delicious food. At an early age, Mankiller learned not to talk about these ceremonies with non-Cherokees. Their white neighbors were quick to condemn Indian religious practices, which they thought were sinful.

A BRIEF HISTORY OF THE CHEROKEE INDIANS

Before contact with non-Indians, the Cherokees were a very large Indian tribe that lived in what is now the American Southeast. There were then probably about 22,000 Cherokees. The tribe's homeland included portions of eight present-day states: Tennessee, Georgia, Alabama, Kentucky, Virginia, West Virginia, North Carolina, and South Carolina. Traditionally, the Cherokees lived in villages located along rivers. Their rich environment provided them with fertile farmland, fishing areas, and hunting grounds teeming with game animals.

The Cherokees first encountered non-Indians in 1540, when Spanish explorer Hernando de Soto led an expedition through their lands. More sustained contact came in the next century, when British traders arrived in Cherokee territory. The Cherokees sided with the British in the American Revolution (1775–1783). As part of their peace treaty with the victorious Americans, the tribe was forced to give up a large area of land. The U.S. government continued to demand land cessions, especially after gold was discovered in Cherokee territory.

In 1830 President Andrew Jackson signed the Indian Removal Act. It initiated the removal policy, by which the federal government sought to move large southeastern tribes, such as the Cherokees, to western lands. Some Cherokees headed west to stake their claims in Indian Territory (now Oklahoma), but most resisted removal. U.S. soldiers eventually began rounding up the Cherokees and forcing them to relocate at gunpoint. A small minority was allowed to remain in the mountains of North Carolina. The rest were compelled to march west under brutal conditions in 1838 and 1839. During the difficult trek, now called the Trail of Tears, as much as one-quarter of the tribal population died.

The survivors slowly rebuilt their lives in Indian Territory. In time,

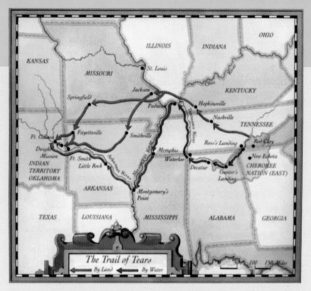

The various routes the Cherokees took during their nineteenth-century relocation to Indian Territory (now Oklahoma).

their towns flourished. They built comfortable houses, created profitable businesses, and established an excellent school system. By the end of the nineteenth century, however, American settlers were again clamoring for access to Cherokee lands. The U.S. Congress reacted by passing the Curtis Act of 1898, which called for the Cherokee government to be dissolved. It also required that the Cherokees' land holdings be broken up into small plots called allotments. Each Cherokee family was assigned an allotment, and the leftover land was opened to white settlement. The majority of the Cherokees' western territory was now in the hands of non-Indians.

The western Cherokees are still known as the Cherokee Nation. They reasserted their right to self-governance in 1971. Today, a principal chief, deputy chief, and tribal council lead the nation once again. The eastern Cherokees now live on the Qualla Boundary in North Carolina. Their formal name is the Eastern Band of Cherokee Indians. In 1950 the federal government formally recognized a third Cherokee tribe: the United Keetoowah Band of Cherokee Indians (UKB). In 2009 the Cherokee Nation had about 280,000 members; the Eastern Band, about 13,400 members; and the UKB, about 13,000 members.

Mankiller also enjoyed visits to Stilwell, the seat of Adair County. On weekends, she and her siblings would go to town to buy treats or to see a movie. The family occasionally attended a Baptist church on Sundays, but, according to Mankiller, they "did not go to Sunday school or learn a great deal about Christianity." Even so, Christmas was a special time in the Mankiller household. No matter how tight their budget, Charley and Irene managed to give the children fruit, candy, and small toys, such as a set of jacks or a jump rope. After a big family dinner, they all went outside and shot guns into the air—a rural version of fireworks.

THE SCHOOL AT ROCKY MOUNTAIN

When she was old enough, Wilma attended a school in the community of Rocky Mountain. The small wooden building, painted bright white, was just large enough for sixty students. Every morning and afternoon, Wilma had to walk the 3 miles (4.8 kilometers) between Mankiller Flats and Rocky Mountain. In the fall, after her father and brother Don returned from Colorado with cash they earned in the broomcorn fields, she looked forward to getting a new pair of leather shoes. Once the winter set in, the shoes made the long, cold walk to and from school a little more bearable.

Mankiller never thought of her family as poor until somebody teased her one day in school. Some other girls had spied her underwear, and they began laughing. Her mother had sewn it out of flour sacks. Her family could not afford to buy other fabric.

In her autobiography, Mankiller also bitterly recalls a few occasions when wealthy white women stopped their cars along the road where

A classroom of Cherokee students poses outside their one-room schoolhouse in the late nineteenth century.

Wilma and her siblings walked to school. They offered the Mankiller children rides and clothing. Mankiller remembered their saying, "Bless your little hearts," a comment that made her bristle. Even as a little girl, she sensed that these white women looked down on her because she was poor and Indian.

In general, young Wilma felt uncomfortable around non-Indians. As she later wrote,

> When I was a little girl, I usually ran off and hid if I spied any white folks coming to our house. I felt shy and embarrassed when I was around non-Indians. I would run to the woods or hide in the attic.

EMBRACING THE CHEROKEE WAY

Wilma felt uncomfortable even around her great aunt, after whom she was named. Aunt Wilma was a white woman married to her father's uncle, George. They were wealthy because oil was discovered on George's land. When Aunt Wilma visited the Mankillers, she always brought them new clothing and other gifts.

Even so, Wilma much preferred the company of her Cherokee relatives. She especially liked Aunt Maggie, who lived nearby. According to Mankiller, "My brother Johnny and I walked to her house with eggs to swap for fresh milk. If we were lucky, Aunt Maggie had a story to tell us. I didn't know it at the time, but Aunt Maggie told stories in the old Cherokee tradition. Some of those tales were frightening and others were not, but all of her stories taught us a lesson of some kind." Wilma also loved Maggie's tales of the rough world of Adair County before 1907, when Oklahoma became a state: "She spoke of outlaws and gunmen and posses and hidden treasure."

From the outside, Mankiller's childhood may have looked like one of deprivation and struggle, but that was never the way it seemed to her. Even if money was scarce, she was always surrounded by friends, family, and a lush countryside that she loved. Growing up in Mankiller Flats, Wilma developed a deep devotion to the place and its people. That devotion not only helped make her youth secure and rewarding. It also shaped her destiny.

CHAPTER TWO

A Cherokee Girl in the City

I N 1956 A GROUP OF OFFICIALS FROM Washington, D.C., went to Mankiller Flats. They worked for the Bureau of Indian Affairs (BIA), the federal agency charged with managing the U.S. government's dealings with American-Indian tribes. The officials met with Charley Mankiller to discuss a new policy called relocation. The goal of this new policy was to persuade American Indians living in rural areas to move to big cities.

Charley listened to what the officials had to say, but he was not interested in relocating his family. After all, Mankiller Flats was the only home his children had ever known. He also remembered the difficult years he had spent in a government-run boarding school. Charley was hesitant to uproot his children as he had been uprooted in his youth.

PROMISE OF A NEW LIFE

The BIA officials persisted, however. They made a good case for relocation. They said that in a city Charley could make a better living than he ever could in rural Oklahoma. They showed him promotional brochures filled with pictures of happy Indian families living in modern apartments equipped with indoor plumbing, electricity, and new appliances. One BIA brochure appealed to Indian parents' sense of responsibility for their families. It read, "If you won't do this much for yourself, at

During the 1950s and 1960s, many American Indian families moved from rural areas to cities through the U.S. government's relocation program.

least do it for the sake of your children." The BIA promised to help Indians find good jobs and comfortable homes in the city.

Charley began to take the BIA's proposal seriously. He talked it over with his friends and his wife Irene. While their parents discussed the matter, the Mankiller children secretly listened by the door. They heard Charley and Irene talk about moving to Chicago, New York, San Francisco, or Detroit—faraway cities Wilma had barely even heard of.

Wilma's parents finally made their decision. With the help of the BIA, they would move the Mankiller family to San Francisco, California. Irene had been against relocating, but eventually she came around to the idea. For Irene, the deciding factor was the fact that her mother was then living in a farm community called Riverbank, which was about 90 miles (144.8 km) away from San Francisco. Even though she did not want to leave her home, Irene welcomed the chance for her children to visit their grandmother regularly.

A MISERABLE JOURNEY

Wilma was distraught by the news. She had never stepped foot out of Oklahoma, so the prospect of moving hundreds of miles away was frightening. But even worse was the idea of leaving Mankiller Flats. She loved her home and had no desire to live anywhere else.

Wilma begged her parents to let her stay behind with friends, but they refused. Then, with her sister Frances, she desperately made plans to run away. But at ten years old, she realized that was impossible. Wilma had no choice but to do what her parents wanted, no matter how much she disagreed with it.

In 1956, just before Wilma's eleventh birthday, the Mankillers piled into a car and headed for the town of Stilwell. As Wilma later

TERMINATION AND RELOCATION

During Wilma Mankiller's youth in the 1950s and 1960s, the U.S. government enacted two new policies regarding American-Indian tribes: termination and relocation. Both policies had the same goals: to disband Indian communities and to assimilate Indians into non-Indian society. The policies were also meant to save money by freeing the U.S. government of its treaty obligations to Indians.

Congress adopted the termination policy in 1953. This policy would terminate, or dissolve, Indian tribes and close down their reservations. Terminated tribes would lose all federal aid, as well as special hunting and fishing rights they had gained by treaty.

Relocation targeted individuals rather than tribes. Under this policy, government officials tried to persuade Indian families to move to large cities. They told the Indians that they could greatly improve their lives by relocating to urban areas. In cities, the officials promised, Indians could find better jobs and housing than they could in their own communities.

Termination and relocation proved disastrous for many Indian people. With the loss of federal aid and reservation lands, most terminated tribes were plunged into poverty and despair. Many relocated Indians found that, contrary to the government's claim, a move to the city did not lead to a better life. Unable to find good jobs, they remained poor but no longer had the social and economic support of friends and family they had known back home.

Even the U.S. government eventually acknowledged the destructiveness of these policies. In the 1970s, both were abandoned in favor of a policy of self-determination. Self-determination gave Indian tribes more say over how federal funds provided to Indians should be spent. Because of this new policy, Indians and their governments gained control over social and economic development programs designed to benefit their tribes.

remembered, "As we drove away, I looked at our house, the store, my school. I took last looks. I wanted to remember it all. I tried to memorize the shapes of the trees, the calls of the animals and birds from the forest. All of us looked out the windows. We did not want to forget anything." In Stilwell, they boarded a train bound for California. The journey took two days and two nights. According to Mankiller, her sister Frances cried the entire way.

COPING WITH CITY LIFE

When the Mankillers arrived in San Francisco, the BIA put them up in a hotel in a rough part of the city. Mankiller said it was "like landing on Mars." The prostitutes roaming the streets and the homeless men sleeping in doorways stunned young Wilma. The glare of neon lights and the sound of traffic assaulted her eyes and ears. All the Mankiller children were terrified by their new surroundings. At night, disturbed by the street noise outside, they huddled under the covers. Mankiller later explained, "We had never heard sirens before. I thought it was some sort of wild creature screaming."

After a few weeks, the Mankillers moved to a small apartment in a Hispanic neighborhood. Wilma's father and brother Don went to work in a rope factory. Even though they worked long hours, their paychecks were hardly enough to keep the family fed. Wilma still felt overwhelmed by the city, but her neighbors tried to help the Mankillers adjust. They taught Wilma how to use a telephone and how to roller-skate on the sidewalk.

Starting school only added to Wilma's misery. From the first day, she felt out of place. During roll call, the other students laughed at her name—a common Cherokee name that no one back in Oklahoma found the least bit funny. Her classmates also teased her about her

Young Wilma Mankiller found it difficult to adjust to living in the bustling city of San Francisco, California.

unfashionable clothes and country accent. Wilma and her sister Linda became so self-conscious that they spent every night reading to each other, trying to learn to pronounce words the way city kids did.

At home, Wilma and Frances liked to talk about Mankiller Flats to keep it fresh in their memories: "We tried to remember where a specific tree was located and how everything looked." Thinking about her old home was the only way Wilma could relieve her anxiety. "There was literally no place for me to run and hide—at least, not at first," she later wrote. "In those early days, when we were all trying to figure out how to get along, there was no real sanctuary for me. . . . We might as well have been on the far side of the moon."

THE MANKILLER NAME

Just about every journalist who interviewed Wilma Mankiller asked her about the same thing: her last name. Mankiller is a fairly common Cherokee surname. It has been in Mankiller's family for at least six generations.

Originally, Mankiller was not a name, but a military title. Each Cherokee village had a Mankiller, who helped protect its residents. There are several famous Mankillers in Cherokee history. One was Outacity (a version of the Cherokee word for "man killer"). A well-respected warrior and tribal leader, he was part of a Cherokee delegation that traveled to London, England, in 1762.

When Wilma was a girl, her father taught her to be proud of her name, although her classmates sometimes made fun of it. Even as an adult, she has had to endure prying questions and sneering remarks from non-Cherokees. In her autobiography, Mankiller explains her method of dealing with the situation: "When someone unknowingly or out of ignorance makes a snide comment about my name, I often resort to humor. I look the person in the eye and say with a straight face that mankiller is actually a well-earned nickname. That usually shuts the person up."

RUNNING AWAY

Wilma's despair only grew worse when the family moved to a house in the suburb of Daly City. Uprooted again, she struggled to make friends at her new school. She was also upset by her changing body. As she grew taller, Wilma felt more awkward than ever. In her autobiography, she recalls,

> I hated what was happening. I hated my body. I hated school. I hated the teachers. I hated the other students. Most of all, I hated the city.

Finally, Wilma felt that she could not stand her life a minute longer. She took her stash of babysitting money, bought a bus ticket to Riverbank, and ran away to the house of her grandmother, Pearl Sitton. When Wilma arrived, Sitton immediately called Charley, who drove out and took his daughter back home.

But Wilma was still determined to get away. During the next few months, she ran away several more times. Tired of retrieving her, her parents agreed to let her live with her grandmother for a year.

FROM THE COUNTRY TO THE CITY

At that time, Sitton lived on a dairy farm owned by her son Floyd. Every morning, Wilma had to get up at five o'clock in the morning to milk the cows and clean the barn. She was so happy in her new setting that she actually enjoyed doing her chores: "Hard work and fresh

Many of Mankiller's happiest days in California were spent with her grandmother on a dairy farm, similar to the one pictured.

air at the farm were so good. We also found time to explore the fields and swim in the creeks."

Wilma also loved spending time with her grandmother. Sitton was strict but fair, and she had an independent streak that Wilma admired. Living with her grandmother, Wilma learned the value of hard work and became more confident in her intelligence and abilities.

After a year, a more self-assured Wilma returned to her parents' home. Her brother Don had since married, leaving the Mankillers without his paycheck. They had to leave their Daly City house for a smaller apartment in the San Francisco neighborhood of Hunters Point. Most of its residents were poor African Americans. There,

Wilma found a circle of girlfriends, who got together to "put on makeup, [fix] our hair, [play] records, and [dance,] pretending we were at a party far away from Hunters Point."

Life was hard in the violent neighborhood. On the streets, gangs of African Americans battled with gangs of Samoan immigrants. The black residents also faced racial prejudice and the gnawing despair that came with poverty. Despite these obstacles, Wilma encountered many people, especially women, who impressed her with their determination to improve their families' lives. In her autobiography, she writes,

> **It takes a certain tenacity, a toughness, to continue on when there is an ever-present worry about whether the old car will work, and . . . wondering if there will be enough to eat. But always, there is hope that the children will receive a good education and have a better life.**

In 1993, before an audience at Sweet Briar College, Mankiller explained the valuable lesson she learned from her time in Hunters Point:

> **What I learned from my experience in living in a community of almost all African-American people is that poor people have a much, much greater capacity for solving their own problems than most people give them credit for.**

FINDING REFUGE

During her teenage years, Wilma also made friends at the San Francisco Indian Center. It was just one of many Indian centers that were established in American cities beginning in the 1960s, when Indians flooded into urban areas because of the relocation policy. Like Wilma, most relocatees were unhappy with their new lives. They missed friends and family from their old communities. Many also felt the BIA had betrayed them. All too often, the good jobs that the BIA promised to relocatees turned out to be low-paying, menial work, and the modern housing the BIA promoted was actually run-down apartments in urban slums.

For Indians disappointed with city life, Indian centers were a refuge. They offered children a safe play space. They gave teenagers a spot to gather for dances and athletic competitions. They provided adults with a place to play cards and bingo or just to visit with one another. Perhaps most important, Indian centers encouraged struggling Indians to get

together, to talk about their problems, and to seek advice from others who could sympathize with their troubles. In this way, Indian centers offered urban Indians support similar to what they had had in their old tribal communities.

For Wilma the Indian center in San Francisco was a godsend. Each school day, she muddled through her class work without enthusiasm, just waiting for the final bell. Wilma then rushed out to catch a city bus bound for the center. There, she spent the rest of the day

When Mankiller was a young adult, many American Indians in California cities were involved in the Indian rights movement.

with her Indian friends—the only people she knew in San Francisco, aside from her family, who could really understand what her life was like. The San Francisco Indian Center was far from Oklahoma, but it gave Mankiller a sense of belonging she had not known since leaving Mankiller Flats. As she walked through its doors each afternoon, she almost felt as though she were coming home.

CHAPTER THREE

Getting Involved

I N THE SUMMER OF 1963, SEVENTEEN-YEAR-OLD Wilma Mankiller graduated from high school. She was thrilled. In her mind, leaving high school "meant no more associating with people I did not like, people who did not like me."

Mankiller made no plans to go to college. As she later explained, "That thought never even entered my head. People in my family did not go to college. They went to work." She quickly found a clerical job. It did not pay much, but still she had more spending money than ever before. Mankiller left her parents' house and moved in with her sister Frances.

LOVE AND MARRIAGE

Mankiller loved her newfound independence, especially after she began dating Hugo Olaya. Hailing from a wealthy family in Ecuador, Olaya came to the United States for his education. When he met Mankiller, he was studying business at San Francisco State College.

The couple had a whirlwind romance. Nearly every night, they went out to eat in fancy restaurants and enjoy the city's nightlife. It was an exciting time for Mankiller. As she later explained, "I was a teenager, dating an exotic South American who was going to college and driving his own car. He was dashing and different and good-looking."

Mankiller did not consider continuing her education after she graduated from high school in 1963. After all, no one in her family had ever gone to college.

Within a few months, Olaya started asking Mankiller to marry him. Mankiller was hesitant, but one night, on a whim, she said yes. Just five days before her eighteenth birthday, the couple flew to Reno, Nevada, for a quick wedding ceremony. While heading off on their honeymoon, Mankiller was already having second thoughts about her decision. Nevertheless, she figured she had to "plunge ahead and make the best of it."

A YOUNG WIFE AND MOTHER

A few months later, Mankiller suddenly became ill. She felt terrible pain in her back and began vomiting whenever she ate. She went to an emergency room, where the doctors gave her two diagnoses. A kidney infection had caused the back pain, but a surprise pregnancy was responsible for the nausea.

In August 1964 Mankiller gave birth to her first daughter, Felicia. Two years later, she had her second, Gina. The family settled down in a comfortable house in San Francisco. Mankiller quit her job and stayed home to raise the children. As she explained, "I kept house, shopped, cooked, and cleaned. I evolved into my role of young wife and mother."

Almost from the start, Mankiller was uneasy with her new life. She had a nice home, two lovely daughters, and a caring husband, yet she was unsatisfied with her day-to-day existence. Mankiller blamed herself for her unhappiness. She later recalled,

> **I had felt there was something wrong with me because I wasn't happy being a traditional housewife.**

Mankiller found some relief in the changing social scene in San Francisco. The city had become a magnet for young and inventive musicians, painters, and writers. Many of them flocked to the district around the intersection of Haight and Ashbury streets. Mankiller liked to take her daughters there and just walk around. They would soak in the exciting atmosphere and thrilling sense of change.

Part of that change was a new willingness, especially on the part of young people, to challenge the political system and the social hierarchy. Many San Franciscans were vocal opponents of the nation's involvement in the Vietnam War (1957–1975). Others were fighting

Mankiller supported the antiwar movement of the 1960s and 1970s, which demanded that the United States withdraw its troops from the country of Vietnam in Southeast Asia.

"IT WAS AN INCREDIBLE TIME"

In January 2009 Wilma Mankiller appeared on *A Conversation With . . .* , a program on Oklahoma's public television station, OETA. During the interview, Mankiller described her youth in San Francisco and explained how it helped shape her life:

> I grew up during a time of great political change in this country, and so there was a huge free speech movement going on at Berkeley [California]. There was a huge antiwar movement going on relative to Vietnam, and a civil rights movement was going full-swing. Native-American people were beginning to stand up and advocate for recognition of treaty rights and tribal sovereignty, and so it was, you know, it was an incredible time. . . . So it was that kind of era where there was change—change was in the air. And a lot of young, just regular, everyday middle-class people, young people were questioning what was going on around them and thinking they may want to do something a little different. So growing up in that kind of environment, where at San Francisco State there were meetings for the early contemporary women's movement—just so many things whirling around, so many things to think about and see and do, [it] had a profound impact on me and my entire family.

for the end of discrimination against the poor and against minorities, such as African Americans and Hispanics.

The more curious Mankiller became about these growing social and political movements, the less comfortable she was at home. A trip to visit friends in a suburban area made it clear to her how unhappy she was:

> The whole time I was there, I felt as if I were suffocating. All around us in the city were people—interesting people—discussing politics, music, theology, world events—but there we were in the suburbs talking about lawn mowers at a house that looked exactly like all the others on the street.

BREAKING FREE

Wanting to learn more about the world, Mankiller began taking college classes. Free to study her favorite subjects, such as literature and sociology, she found that she liked school for the first time in her life. Mankiller also enjoyed the sense of independence she felt: "I wanted to set my own limits and control my destiny. I began to have dreams about more freedom and independence, and I finally came to understand that I did not have to live a life based on someone else's dream."

The emerging women's movement bolstered Mankiller's feelings. Many of the women Mankiller knew began talking about their dissatisfaction with strict social roles, which defined them only as someone's wife or someone's mother. Suddenly, Mankiller no longer felt it was wrong that she wanted to be more than a housewife. Her urge to get out of the house and into the world annoyed her husband. As Mankiller became more independent, her relationship with Olaya became increasingly strained.

Mankiller's new perspective inspired her to renew her ties to the San Francisco Indian Center. In the 1960s American Indians, like other minorities, fought for their rights and called for an end to unjust treatment by the federal government. Some of the most militant activists in this movement frequented the Indian center. Mankiller found their passion exciting, yet she was unsure about whether she wanted to fully commit herself to their cause.

PLANNING A PROTEST

By early 1969 the frustration of activists at the San Francisco Indian Center had reached a boiling point. They decided to do something to get the attention of the federal government and to express their demands for change—not tomorrow or some other time in the future, but today. The activists were determined to stage a protest so bold that no one could ignore it.

They focused their plans on Alcatraz, an island in the San Francisco Bay. Alcatraz had been the home of a federal prison where the most notorious criminals were sent. The facility had been shut down in 1963. Since then, San Francisco's city government had been considering an array of ideas for what to do with the island. Finally, in the fall of 1969, the city approved a proposal by an entrepreneur who wanted to turn Alcatraz into a multi-million-dollar shopping complex and tourist attraction.

The Indians of San Francisco came up with their own plan for Alcatraz. They decided to take over the island and to declare it Indian property. Their justification for the takeover was the Treaty of Fort Laramie. The U.S. government had negotiated this treaty with several bands of the Sioux and the Arapahos in 1868. The document included a provision that allowed any adult male who was a member of one of the signing tribes to claim a homestead on abandoned or unused federal property.

The Indian activists were not really interested in homesteading on Alcatraz. Their planned seizure of the island was meant as a symbolic gesture. It would protest all the times the U.S. government had illegally or unjustly taken over Indian property.

LANDING ON ALCATRAZ

The takeover of Alcatraz was to take place in the summer of 1970. But on October 28, 1969, a fire swept through the San Francisco Indian Center and destroyed the facility. San Francisco's Indians were furious; many believed the center had been a target of arson. The city government tried to calm the situation by looking for an alternative space for the center. The Indian activists, however, were not pleased with any of the city's offers.

With tempers at a fever pitch, a few activists decided they had to carry out the Alcatraz protest early. A small group of Indians, mostly local students, set off for the island on a chartered boat on November 9, 1969. They symbolically claimed Alcatraz as Indian property and returned to San Francisco the same day.

On November 20 a larger group staged another Alcatraz takeover.

This time, about eighty Indian men, women, and children, led by Mohawk activist Richard Oakes, arrived on the island. The group called themselves the Indians of All Tribes. They took food, water, sleeping bags, and other supplies with them. They intended to stay for as long as possible.

IN THE NEWS

The Alcatraz takeover soon made the national news. As the activists dug in for a long siege, they found a host of supporters. Indians from all over the United States were inspired by their actions. Many headed out to California to join in the protest. Indian protesters came and went, but at times the population of the island grew as high as a thousand.

Many non-Indians were also sympathetic to the Indians' grievances. Across the country, church groups, labor unions, and even Girl Scout and Boy Scout troops collected money, food, and clothing to send to the protesters. Celebrities also lent their support. Actresses Jane Fonda and Candice Bergen, comedian Jonathan Winters, and talk show host Merv Griffin were among the stars who traveled to Alcatraz. As the months passed, their presence helped keep the occupation in the news. The U.S. Coast Guard tried to blockade Alcatraz, but a steady stream of boats carrying reporters and photographers continued to make its way to the island.

Among the Indians who joined the protest were four of Mankiller's brothers and sisters. Wilma herself did not participate in the occupation, however. Instead, she stayed on the mainland and volunteered to help organize fund-raising efforts at the Indian center to keep the Alcatraz protest going. Even though she was working behind the scenes, Alcatraz completely changed Mankiller's life. "The occupation of Alcatraz excited me like nothing ever had before," she later

Dancing in ceremonial dress, these Indian activists, photographed in 1969, were energized by the takeover of Alcatraz Island by the Indians of All Tribes.

explained. She had always been outraged by the mistreatment of American Indians, but now she became confident that she and other Indians could do something about it if they worked together. According to Mankiller,

> **The Alcatraz experience nurtured a sense among us that anything was possible—even, perhaps, justice for native people.**

The occupation continued for nineteen months. It had more than succeeded in its goals. The Indians of All Tribes had shown the world that they were angry about federal Indian policies and were willing to fight to see them changed. It also inspired Indian activists throughout the nation to see themselves not as a degraded people, but as a powerful force that could compel the U.S. government to improve the lives of all Indians. As Mankiller later remembered, "The entire Alcatraz occupation was such an important period for me. Every day that passed seemed to give me more self-respect and sense of pride."

MAKING A DIFFERENCE

During the Alcatraz protest, the Mankiller family experienced a personal tragedy. Wilma's father had fallen seriously ill from polycystic kidney disease, which he likely inherited from his father. In February 1971 Charley Mankiller died at the age of fifty-six. The family took his body back to Adair County. His burial there comforted Wilma: "There was something very natural about laying him to rest in that ground near people he loved. It was so peaceful, and I knew the trees would protect him."

Mankiller tried to cope with her grief by throwing herself into working for Indian causes. After the Alcatraz protest ended, she became a volunteer at the Native American Youth Center in East Oakland, California. The center gave Indian students and dropouts a safe place where they could come together after school hours. Mankiller later wrote, "I had no idea what I was doing when I became involved at the youth center, but I learned quickly—on the job."

Eventually becoming the director of the center, Mankiller created educational programs that helped Indian children develop pride in themselves. To fund the programs, she taught herself how to write proposals for grants—cash awards given by a charitable organization to fund worthwhile projects. She also hustled to gather volunteers to work at the center. Mankiller even visited a corner bar catering to Indians to solicit help and money to keep the center going. Mankiller's experiences at the youth center gave her faith in Indians' abilities to change their own communities:

> **[I]t was in Oakland . . . I formed a belief that poor people, particularly poor American Indian people, have a lot more potential and many more answers to problems than they are ever given a chance to realize.**

At the same time, Mankiller became involved in the efforts of the Pit River Indians to reclaim their homeland. During the 1960s, this northern California tribe was in a heated legal battle with the Pacific Gas and Electric Company for control of millions of acres of land. When Mankiller saw a television news report about the struggle, she became determined to help. At the time, she knew little about treaty rights and laws governing American-Indian tribes, so she set out to learn everything could. For the five years she worked as a volunteer for the Pit River Tribe, she studied the complex legal issues surrounding ongoing Indian land claims.

During that time, Mankiller occasionally visited the Pit River leaders. She enjoyed spending time in the tribe's communities, which made her recall her youth in Mankiller Flats. As she later wrote,

> **They were rural people—a very gutsy tribe just trying to get back what was rightfully theirs. Something about them reminded me of the Cherokees.**

ON HER OWN

The satisfaction Mankiller found in her volunteer work made one thing clear: living as a housewife as her husband wanted her to, she would never be happy in her marriage. In 1974 she asked Olaya for a divorce. At first, Olaya was angry, but he eventually agreed. During her marriage, Mankiller had called herself Wilma Olaya. But once the divorce came through, she proudly reclaimed the Mankiller name.

Olaya did not always pay child support, so Mankiller took a job as a social worker to make ends meet. Olaya continued to visit with his daughters. One day, he picked up nine-year-old Gina for a trip to the circus. Then he fled with the girl. Mankiller did not see Gina again for almost a year.

After Olaya returned Gina, Mankiller lived in fear that he would try the same stunt again. To get away from Olaya, she decided to take the girls to Oklahoma for the summer of 1976. Living in Mankiller Flats was hard for Felicia and Gina at first. The city girls had trouble adjusting to a rural setting without modern conveniences, such as electricity and indoor plumbing. Mankiller was thrilled to be back home, however. The sights, sounds, and smells of Mankiller Flats still felt familiar. She had spent the last twenty years of her life in San Francisco, but somehow she felt as though she had never left Oklahoma.

After a few weeks, Mankiller and her daughters returned to California. As they settled into their old lives, Mankiller knew what she had to do. One way or another, she had to go back to Mankiller Flats—this time for good.

CHAPTER FOUR

Going Home

I N THE SUMMER OF 1977 WILMA MANKILLER loaded her daughters and all her possessions into a rented truck. Driving away, they said goodbye to California and headed toward a new life in Oklahoma. As Mankiller later explained,

> **I had to go back to stay. Back to the land of my birth, back to the soil and trees my grandfather had touched, back to the animals and birds whose calls I had memorized as a girl when we packed our things and left on a westbound train so very long ago.**

Mankiller's immediate plan was to stay with her mother, who had earlier decided to move back to Mankiller Flats. "When we arrived at my mother's place," Mankiller recalled in her autobiography, "I had twenty dollars to my name, no car, no job, and few, if any prospects. But we were happy."

While the girls struggled to adjust to their new home, Mankiller set out to find work. Given her experiences with tribal organizations in California, Mankiller's first idea was to get a job with the government of the Cherokee Nation. She kept filling out applications for open positions, but over and over

The natural beauty of Oklahoma helped lure Mankiller back to her childhood home.

THE MODERN CHEROKEE GOVERNMENT

When Oklahoma became a state in 1907, the United States all but dissolved the Cherokees' government. The Cherokees were still led by a principal chief, but he was appointed by the U.S. president, not elected by the Cherokee people.

The situation changed in the 1970s, when the federal government adopted a new policy called self-determination. It allowed Indian tribes to set up their own governments. The Cherokees held their first election in 1971. For principal chief, the voters chose William W. Keeler, who had held the post as an appointee since 1949. Keeler assembled a committee to write a new constitution for the tribe.

Keeler retired after one term and was succeeded by Ross Swimmer. During Swimmer's administration, the new constitution was ratified in 1976. It established a three-part government similar to that of the United States. The executive branch consisted of a principal chief and a deputy chief, who were elected every four years. The legislative branch was made up of a tribal council, whose members were also elected by the people. The judicial branch included a three-member judicial tribunal appointed by the principal chief.

In 2006 the Cherokee Nation adopted a new constitution. Under its terms, the tribal council was expanded from fifteen to nineteen members. The judicial branch now includes the Cherokee Nation Supreme Court, which resolves disputes over the interpretation of the constitution, and the Cherokee Nation District Court, which hears all other cases.

she was told she was overqualified or just not quite right for the job. Frustrated, one day she marched into the nation's employment office and said,

> ## I want to work! Whatever you have, please let me try it. I need to go to work!

WORKING FOR THE CHEROKEES

Mankiller's boldness paid off. She was hired to work as an economic stimulus coordinator. It was her job to help young Cherokees get into college programs to study environmental science or health care. Once they obtained their degrees, the students were expected to return to the Cherokee Nation and use their training to help the Cherokee people.

Mankiller's work in San Francisco made her seem perfect for the job. But, according to Mankiller, she

> ## soon found that things were not done in quite the same way in the Cherokee Nation.

She was used to working hands-on and organizing programs however she saw fit. But the Cherokee government was a large bureaucracy with distinct rules about how she should do her job. Even though she found it difficult to adjust, Mankiller threw herself into the job. She worked long hours and weekends. As she struggled to prove herself, many of her co-workers warmed to her unortho-dox working methods. As Greg Combs, an attorney who worked with Mankiller on several projects, explained, her experiences in California meant that

> ## . . . she came equipped with ideas that other people didn't have.

In 1979 Mankiller became a program development specialist. She excelled at the job, particularly because of one important skill. In San Francisco, she had taught herself how to write successful grant proposals. She now used this talent to obtain grants for underfunded tribal projects. During her two years in the job, she helped create and fund a wide variety of programs that aided senior citizens, improved health care, and helped children in need.

After returning to Oklahoma, Mankiller decided to take the remaining classes she needed to earn a college degree. In 1977 she received a bachelor of science degree in Indian affairs from Flaming Rainbow University in Stilwell. Mankiller then decided to enter the graduate program in community planning at the University of Arkansas, located just over the state line in the town of Fayetteville.

Mankiller was pleased with her life. She was proud of her academic success and exciting new career. She was also happy about the home she had made for her daughters. At first, the girls had mixed feelings about settling in a rural community. As they made friends and adjusted to their new school, however, they were growing to love Mankiller Flats almost as much as their mother did.

DISASTER ON A COUNTRY ROAD

Just as everything seemed to be going her way, Mankiller had a disquieting experience. On the night of November 8, 1979, she heard a rustling in the trees. Suddenly, her house was surrounded by owls. Many Cherokees believe that if an owl comes too close to a person's house, it is an omen that something bad is about to happen. As Mankiller recalled,

> **I am not someone who experiences premonitions or visions . . . [but] a kind of uneasiness did wash over me.**

The following morning, Mankiller was driving on a country road toward Tahlequah. Just a few miles from her home, she headed up a hill. Suddenly, an oncoming car moved into her lane as the driver tried to pass two slow-moving vehicles. Mankiller tried to swerve to safety, but it was too late. The car struck hers.

An ambulance soon arrived and carried Mankiller's battered body to the hospital. She was covered with blood. Her face and right leg were completely crushed. But as she drifted in and out of consciousness, she felt strangely "wonderful." Believing she was about to die, she

> **experienced a tremendous sense of peacefulness and warmth. It was probably the most profound experience I have ever had.**

Mankiller then thought of Felicia and Gina and

> ## made an unconscious choice to return to life.

Mankiller stayed in the hospital for the next eight weeks. She endured a series of surgeries, most intended to save her right leg, which her doctors feared they would have to amputate. All the while, Mankiller was in excruciating physical pain. However, her worst moment came when she learned the identity of the other driver, who had not survived the accident. It was Sherry Morris, one of Mankiller's closest friends in Oklahoma. When Morris's husband told her the horrible news, Mankiller screamed and wept. She felt terrible guilt for surviving, when her friend Sherry did not.

SURVIVING ILLNESS AND INJURY

At last Mankiller was allowed to return home, but her recovery was far from over. She was confined to a wheelchair and unable to do anything without help. Mankiller's mother and sister Linda took care of Felicia and Gina while Wilma focused on getting better. For weeks, she concentrated on learning to walk again. At the same time, she struggled with her mental health and tried hard not to get depressed over her troubles.

> ## I fell back on my Cherokee ways and adopted what our elders call 'a Cherokee approach' to life,

Mankiller later said. She cultivated what the Cherokees call "being of good mind," a way of thinking positively no matter what difficulties arise.

In early 1980, just as she was able to walk without crutches, Mankiller started noticing some new and strange symptoms. She began seeing double and started losing muscle control. Soon, her hands were so weak that she could not hold a toothbrush. She consulted several specialists, but none of her doctors could figure out what was wrong. In time, she could no longer stand or even hold her head up. All she could do was lie down with her eyes closed and prepare herself for death.

After seven months of agony, she happened to see a televised telethon to benefit the Muscular Dystrophy Association. The show featured a woman suffering from a form of muscular dystrophy called myasthenia gravis. As the woman listed her symptoms, Mankiller suddenly thought, "My God! That's what I have!"

Mankiller was right. Within a week, she was diagnosed with the disease. In November 1980 she traveled to a hospital in Tulsa, Oklahoma, for more medical tests. There, Mankiller decided to do everything she could to beat her illness. She agreed to have surgery to remove her thymus gland and to start a drug program of powerful steroids. The treatment was a success. Her muscle control returned in just a few weeks.

By early 1981, Mankiller was back at work. She was more driven than ever to do all she could to help the Cherokees. She was especially concerned with the poorest tribe members. Mankiller still remembered how, when she was young, her family often had to struggle just to get by. These thoughts fueled what Mankiller called a "healthy anger." She was determined to find new ways to lift Cherokee families out of poverty.

THE BELL PROJECT

That year, Ross Swimmer, principal chief of the Cherokee Nation, created a new government department to concentrate on community development. He asked Mankiller to work in the department, which she later ended up directing. Swimmer knew about Mankiller's grant-writing skills. He was confident she would be able to raise the funds needed to make the department a success.

Mankiller's biggest challenge in the job was the Bell project. Located about 10 miles (16 km) from Mankiller Flats, Bell was one of the poorest communities in Oklahoma. Many of its 350 residents lived in broken-down houses with no running water. The goal of the project was to improve the living conditions in Bell. Mankiller was charged with organizing the construction of a water line, the repair of old houses, and the building of some new homes.

Mankiller not only looked for grants to fund the community revitalization project, but also asked Bell residents to help. During her years in San Francisco, Mankiller had become convinced that poor people were willing and able to improve their communities if only they had access to the money and expert help they needed to do so. She applied this self-help approach to the Bell project. She told the people of Bell that her department would provide the funds and management skills, but they would have to provide the labor.

Some Cherokees lacked confidence in the Bell project. They predicted that Mankiller and her new ideas would fail to produce anything worthwhile. A few families in Bell shared their skepticism and refused to do any work. Mankiller quickly dropped them from the project and provided no improvements to their homes.

The vast majority of Bell residents, however, were eager to pitch in. Working together, they laid 16 miles (25.7 km) of water pipe. They repaired about twenty houses, as well as Bell's community center. They also built twenty-five new energy-efficient homes. With Mankiller's leadership and the grant money she raised, the people of Bell transformed their community.

The Bell project was a terrific success. It also provided the Cherokees with a model for how to improve other struggling communities. For Mankiller, the project confirmed her beliefs about her own people. She was convinced that, if all the Cherokees worked together, they could do great things.

CHAPTER FIVE

Entering
Tribal Politic

I N EARLY 1983 PRINCIPAL CHIEF SWIMMER asked to speak with Mankiller. He was very pleased with her work on the Bell project, but that was not what he wanted to talk about. Instead, he had a proposition for her. He was preparing to run for reelection. Swimmer wanted Mankiller to join his ticket and run for the office of deputy chief. It was an important position. In the Cherokee Nation, the offices of principal chief and deputy chief are the equivalent of president and vice president in the United States.

Mankiller was stunned. She saw herself as a community organizer, not as a politician.

> **I couldn't imagine myself in a political office and having to go out and sell myself like a tube of toothpaste or something,**

she later wrote. Without hesitation, Mankiller told Swimmer that, although she was honored, she would have to decline his offer. She could not see herself as being elected, much less serving in office.

WHY MANKILLER?

Mankiller was right in thinking she was a peculiar choice. She and Swimmer shared the belief that the best way of improving

The Cherokee tribal council approved the official seal of the Cherokee Nation in 1871. September 6, 1839, was the date the western Cherokees adopted their constitution.

Cherokee communities was to help the Cherokees help themselves. But on just about every other political policy, the two disagreed. Like many Cherokees, Swimmer was a conservative Republican, while Mankiller was a liberal Democrat. Their political philosophies were so far apart that Swimmer and Mankiller made little sense as running mates.

But Swimmer was facing some unusual problems. A year earlier, he had been diagnosed with lymphatic cancer. He had been treated successfully, but many of his political allies had abandoned him because they thought he was too ill to lead. He also had lost the support of his deputy chief, Perry Wheeler. In 1982 Wheeler had made it clear that instead of running again for deputy chief, he wanted to challenge Swimmer in the principal chief race.

With so many of his old political friends against him, Swimmer was forced to approach someone outside his immediate circle. Mankiller suspected Swimmer had thought of her because he knew she was "honest with money and dedicated to the tribe." He probably was also impressed with the management skills she had displayed while working on the Bell project. Swimmer also knew that he would be spending a good deal of time discussing Indian causes with lawmakers in Washington, D.C. Mankiller seemed like a good person to entrust with managing the day-to-day business of running the Cherokee Nation while he was away.

JOINING THE RACE

After Mankiller flatly turned down Swimmer's offer, she began to rethink what she had done. Was she really such an unlikely choice to be deputy chief? Wouldn't the position give her the power to make real and important changes in the lives of the Cherokees?

While she was wrestling with these questions, she traveled to a rural Cherokee community. There, she spied "a very sad scene." One family was so poor that it was living in an abandoned bus without a roof. When she saw that family, Mankiller thought about all the things they and many other struggling Cherokees needed: decent housing, access to health care, better jobs, and the opportunity to pursue an education. The family in the bus changed Mankiller's mind. As she later wrote,

> **I knew that if I did not act, I would no longer have any right to talk about or criticize the people who held tribal offices.**

Mankiller told Swimmer that she was ready to join him in the campaign. Swimmer officially supported Mankiller, but the principal chief and deputy chief races were separate. She and Swimmer would have to win their respective races if both were to assume office. Furthermore, a candidate had to get more than 50 percent of the vote to win the election. If none of the candidates for a race received that many votes, the top two candidates would have to face each other in a runoff.

Two candidates challenged Mankiller in the deputy chief race. One was J. B. Dreadfulwater, who had been a member of the Cherokee tribal council. The other was Agnes Cowan, who served as director of the tribe's bilingual cultural center. In 1975 Cowan became the first woman ever elected to the tribal council. Four year later, she ran for deputy chief but was defeated.

BELOVED WOMAN NANCY WARD

During her political career, people often compared Wilma Mankiller to the Cherokee leaders once known by the title *Ghigau*, or Beloved Woman. In traditional Cherokee society, Beloved Woman was the highest honor the Cherokees could grant a woman.

The last known Beloved Woman was Nanye'hi, also known as Nancy Ward (c. 1738–c. 1822). Ward grew up in a Cherokee village near what is now Knoxville, Tennessee. When she was still in her teens, she accompanied her husband into battle against the Creek Indians. While he fired his gun at the enemy, Ward stood by his side, yelled words of encouragement, and handed him bullets. During the fight, Ward's husband was shot and killed. She then grabbed his gun and took his place in the battle. In the end, the Cherokees were victorious, and they credited Ward for their triumph. As a reward, they named her a Beloved Woman.

It was not a meaningless title. Being a Beloved Woman carried with it hefty responsibilities. Ward was now permitted to attend the Cherokee Council, an honor usually reserved for male leaders. She was also charged with overseeing the preparation of Black Drink. Warriors drank this special tea to give them strength before going into battle.

During the American Revolution, Ward played the role of peacemaker. The Cherokees officially sided with the British, but Ward wanted to contain the bloodshed. Several times,

This map shows how the boundaries of the Cherokees' homeland in the Southeast changed over time. The red area marks the current homeland of the eastern Cherokees.

she warned American settlers about impending Cherokee raids. After the Americans won the war, she helped negotiate the tribe's first treaty with the United States. Ward was asked to deliver a speech at the end of the negotiations. She told the crowd that the Cherokees warriors were "rejoic[ing] that we have peace, and we hope the chain of friendship will never be broken."

Ward felt less friendly toward Americans in the decades that followed. American settlers took control of more and more Cherokee land. Federal officials even talked of relocating the Cherokees. Ward became appalled by what was happening to the Cherokee homeland, especially after the United States gained control of her home village of Chota. Ward spent her final years running a successful inn in eastern Tennessee. When she died in about 1822, relatives claimed that a white light shone from her body and floated back to Chota.

A TOUGH CAMPAIGN

Mankiller's campaign got off to a slow start. She sent out a pile of invitations to her first campaign event, but only five people came out to hear her speech—and three of them were her own relatives. Mankiller decided that she needed to go to the people instead of waiting for them to come to her.

Again drawing on her background as a community organizer, she gathered a small group of volunteers to spread the word about her campaign. Their leader was her friend Charlie Soap, a Cherokee Nation employee she got to know while working on the Bell project. Mankiller and her supporters went door-to-door and sold her candidacy to anyone who would listen. Soap, who was fluent in the Cherokee language, was especially effective in touting Mankiller to older, more traditional Cherokees.

When she announced that she was running for deputy chief, Mankiller was forced to quit her job. The tribe had a rule that no candidate for office could work for the Cherokee Nation. Even though Mankiller was strapped financially, she poured all her savings into her campaign. As Mankiller once noted, running for office in the second-largest American-Indian tribe was similar to running for Congress. It required funds for print and television advertisements, billboards, and large campaign rallies.

THE GENDER ISSUE

From the start, Mankiller was sure that fellow Cherokees would challenge her stances on political issues. After all, many rural Cherokees were conservatives like Swimmer. The liberal politics she had embraced in San Francisco seemed a little out of the mainstream in the Cherokee Nation in the 1980s.

In her autobiography, Mankiller writes that, to her surprise,

> [n]o one challenged me on those issues, not once. Instead, I was challenged mostly because of one fact—I am female. The election became an issue of gender.

As she explains, "I heard all sorts of things—some people claimed that my running for office was an affront to God. Others said having a female run our tribe would make the Cherokees the laughingstock of the tribal world. I heard it all." She decided just to ignore that line of attack. She recalled a saying:

> If you argue with a fool, someone passing by will not be able to tell who is the fool and who is not.

Dreadfulwater made gender a major issue in the campaign. He claimed he was the best candidate because he was the only man running. Dreadfulwater spoke out against both Mankiller and Cowan. He claimed that neither was qualified for the position of deputy chief because no woman could be a successful leader of the Cherokees. Only a small minority of Cherokees shared Dreadfulwater's views, but those people tended to voice their opinions loudly and often.

FACING CRITICISM

Mankiller's critics had several other reasons for opposing her in addition to her gender. Both Cowan and Dreadfulwater claimed Mankiller was too inexperienced. They were correct in the sense that Mankiller was new to Cherokee politics. In her work for the Cherokee Nation, however, Mankiller had proved herself to be a talented organizer and manager. The other candidates also branded her as an outsider. Even though she had grown up in Mankiller Flats, the thirty-seven-year-old Mankiller had spent twenty years in San Francisco. Some Cherokees wondered if she knew the tribe and its needs as well as longtime residents Cowan and Dreadfulwater.

Probably the most ridiculous criticism leveled at Mankiller involved her clothing choices. Before running for deputy chief, she usually wore jeans and cowboy boots—comfortable clothes that made sense when she was working on outdoor construction projects. Once she hit the campaign trail, however, Swimmer's supporters pushed her to dress more professionally. Mankiller wrote Swimmer with a wry promise to work on her appearance:

> **I will try to look like I have at least considered the question of whether certain colors go well together.**

No matter what Mankiller did, some people in Swimmer's camp refused to support her. Many of his associates were angry that he had chosen her to run for deputy chief instead of Gary Chapman, a council member and close friend of Swimmer's. According to Mankiller's autobiography, Chapman, while serving as Swimmer's campaign manager, spread false rumors that Mankiller had been campaigning in bars. Some members of Swimmer's team were even spotted handing out campaign literature for Dreadfulwater.

Mankiller had to deal with hate mail and even threats of violence. At one campaign rally, someone slashed the tires of her car. When she rode in a parade, she saw a young man position his finger and thumb to make a gun, which he then pointed and "shot" at her. Mankiller refused to let him rattle her and continued waving to the crowd.

> # I never even blinked....
> # I just calmly looked away.

AT THE POLLS

A long, contentious campaign season finally drew to an end. When the Cherokees went to the polls, they reelected Swimmer to his third term as principal chief. In the race for deputy chief, Mankiller won the most votes, but she did not get enough to prevent a runoff election with the second-highest vote getter, Agnes Cowan.

Dreadfulwater had come in last. The majority of Cherokee voters had rejected his theory that women were unfit to lead. With a runoff pitting Mankiller against Cowan, the tribe was now sure to elected its first female deputy chief.

Cowan was a formidable opponent. She had far more political experience than Mankiller. But she also had a tendency to say exactly what was on her mind. Some people found her brutal honesty off-putting.

It was difficult to predict which candidate the voters would choose, but in the end, they selected Mankiller. Those who voted for Mankiller largely fell into two categories: rural Cherokees who admired her work as community development director or strong Swimmer supporters who were swayed by his endorsement.

A NEW DEPUTY CHIEF

Mankiller officially became deputy chief of the Cherokee Nation on August 14, 1983. To her disappointment, however, the ugliness of the campaign did not disappear after she took office. One of her primary roles was to preside over the fifteen-member tribal council. At her first meeting, a male council member began talking over her whenever she started to speak. Before the next meeting, she had the council members' microphones rewired. She was then able to turn down the volume on the microphone of anyone who tried to dominate the proceedings.

None of the council members supported Mankiller. She had assumed that after the election, they would be able to work together. Mankiller especially had high hopes that she could win over the three female members of the council. As ardent allies of Gary Chapman, however, they saw Mankiller as a political enemy. While facing the hostility of the council, Mankiller also had to deal with the presence of Swimmer. He often sat in on council meetings, which Mankiller felt undermined her authority.

Early on in her tenure as deputy chief, she professed to having "mixed emotions" about her new job. She had assumed that being deputy chief would allow her to help the Cherokees who needed help most. Now she feared that she had gained a job title but had lost the chance to promote the projects that meant the most to her.

After a rocky start, Mankiller slowly began to find her way. Without the support of the council, she could have little impact on the policies of the Cherokee government. Instead, she focused on getting involved in the forty programs that the Cherokee Nation operated. The programs' functions ranged from running health clinics to supervising new housing construction to providing assistance to the elderly. As before, Mankiller favored programs designed to help Cherokees help themselves. As she explained,

> [T]he projects that we've always done best are projects we do ourselves. The best way to build an economy for us is to build locally controlled, locally developed businesses where the decisions are made locally.

CHAPTER SIX

Changing Minds

B Y SEPTEMBER 1985, JUST AS MANKILLER was finally adjusting to her role as deputy chief, Principal Chief Swimmer told her some surprising news. President Ronald Reagan had chosen him to head the Bureau of Indian Affairs. Swimmer had accepted the post and planned to move to Washington, D.C.

Swimmer's new post meant a big change not only in his life, but also in Mankiller's. According to the Cherokee constitution, if the principal chief resigned, the deputy chief took over his job. With Swimmer leaving, Mankiller would become the principal chief of the Cherokee Nation—the first woman ever to hold that position.

The job of principal chief was extremely challenging. As Mankiller once described it, it was

> **something like running a big corporation and a little country at the same time.**

The chief headed a government that employed about 1,200 people and had an annual budget of more than $75 million.

A NEW PRINCIPAL CHIEF

After Swimmer publicly announced his plans, he spent most of his time in Washington. He gave Mankiller little guidance as

When Principal Chief Ross Swimmer was appointed the head of the Bureau of Indian Affairs in Washington, D.C., Mankiller, then deputy chief, took over his job.

she stepped into her new role. His only instructions for her were a list of important issues and problems facing the Cherokees. It took up a single sheet of paper. On the day she was sworn into office, Swimmer called to wish Mankiller luck. During the first year of her administration, Swimmer and Mankiller spoke just one other time.

From her first day on the job, Mankiller was largely on her own. She struggled to prepare herself for the daunting work she knew lay ahead. Publicly she appeared confident, but privately she worried that she was not ready to be principal chief.

One of her first orders of business was to end rumors that she was planning on firing tribal employees. At her public swearing-in ceremony, she delivered a speech reassuring the Cherokees that she intended to make no such sweeping changes. Instead, she promised to proceed with the agenda of the Swimmer administration, although she wanted to increase the funding available for social programs and economic development.

Another immediate challenge was dealing with the question of who would take over her old job of deputy chief. The Cherokee constitution left the choice up to the tribal council. Mankiller learned that some council members were promoting Gary Chapman, one of her most vocal critics, for the job. As Mankiller later explained, "I knew that if he obtained the position, he would oppose me at every opportunity." Mankiller instead wanted a councilman named John Ketcher to be deputy chief. She believed that they could work well together and that he could keep the council from trying to undermine her projects.

On December 14, 1985, Mankiller and the tribal council met to choose the deputy chief. Five of the fifteen council members nominated themselves for the job. After four rounds of voting, the council was split between two candidates—Chapman and Ketcher. The council members asked Mankiller for her recommendation. She told them she wanted Ketcher to win. Bowing to the wishes of the new principal chief, Chapman withdrew his name from consideration, and the council elected Ketcher.

MANKILLER AND THE MEDIA

While adjusting to the demands of her new job, Mankiller was inundated with requests for interviews. It was not just local reporters who were clamoring for Mankiller's attention. Many national news and television reporters were interested in her story. Even before Mankiller had taken the oath of office, *People* magazine ran a glowing profile of the Cherokees' new leader.

Why did Mankiller attract so much media attention? There were several reasons, some trivial, some significant. Perhaps the silliest was her unusual name. Reporters inevitably asked her about it. Tired of having to address the same question over and over, Mankiller took to joking about her name. She would often say, "I earned it," and let them wonder what she meant.

Another reason reporters wanted to talk with Mankiller was an increased interest by all Americans in American-Indian history and culture. The Indian rights movement, sparked in part by the Alcatraz takeover, had attracted national attention to the issues concerning contemporary Indian peoples. Before the 1970s, non-Indian Americans often ignored Indian groups or dismissed them as relics of the past. But as Indians became more public with their grievances and demands, non-Indians came to understand that Indians were modern people with a fascinating cultural heritage. This understanding inspired an industry of articles, books, and movies purporting to tell how Indians lived today.

Mankiller's gender also helped make her newsworthy. In the 1980s, women were rising to higher levels of prominence in the work world than ever before. Magazines were filled with stories of women's "firsts." For instance, during the 1980s, Sally Ride became the first American female astronaut to travel to space, and Geraldine Ferraro became the first American woman to run for vice president. Mankiller's rise to power precisely fit the mold for this type of story. Reporters were always trying to dub Mankiller the first female Indian leader. Mankiller and her press office were careful to correct them, because in the past and present, women had led a number of tribes. For accuracy's sake, they made sure that reporters instead referred to Mankiller as the first female chief of a major modern Indian tribe.

For the most part, however, media figures wanted to tell Mankiller's story because she had a terrific story to tell. Her impoverished childhood, her struggles adjusting to the city, her involvement with Alcatraz, her return to her roots, her recovery from a life-threatening car accident and illness, and her unlikely and unexpected rise in politics—everything in her biography added up to a dramatic tale. Her triumph over horrendous physical challenges and subsequent emergence as a history-making leader made her biography not just compelling, but inspirational.

The interest in Mankiller could have faded after the first few interviews, but her personal charm and good humor kept reporters coming back. At first Mankiller was a little overwhelmed by the media attention, but she quickly learned how to deal with the press. She became adept at telling her story in plain language and emphasizing the parts that most intrigued readers and viewers. Mankiller also learned how to use her biography as a way of talking about the Cherokees, their history, and their current struggles. She was thus able to use the attention focused on her to gain more visibility for the issues most important to her tribe.

TROUBLES WITH THE TRIBAL COUNCIL

Mankiller was quickly becoming a national figure, but her new fame did nothing to improve her relationship with the Cherokee tribal council. Several council members were critical of her efforts to improve the tribe's housing and health care systems. They also cried foul after she married her longtime friend Charlie Soap in October 1986. Soap had a job with the Cherokee Nation. Mankiller's critics demanded that he quit so that his wife could not show him any favoritism. Soap did not resign until January 1987, at which point he was eligible for retirement benefits.

At that time, Mankiller was mulling over whether she would run for reelection. She had no illusions about her chances. Mankiller had enough opponents on the tribal council that the campaign was sure to be rough. She asked her family and friends for advice. Some of her friends—and even some of her political allies, including former principal chief Swimmer—told her not to run. They acknowledged that most Cherokees had come to accept Mankiller as their chief while she was filling out Swimmer's term. Even so, they did not think that a majority of voters would elect her to the most powerful position in the tribe.

Mankiller grew weary listening to these naysayers: "Finally, I told Charlie that if one more family came down the road and told me not to run, I was going to run for sure. That is just what happened."

Her joke aside, Mankiller made her decision after talking with the other potential candidates. None seemed to share her goals for the Cherokee Nation. The only way those goals would

FEMALE TRAILBLAZERS IN TRIBAL POLITICS

In 1985 Wilma Mankiller became internationally famous when she became the first female principal chief of the Cherokee Nation. But Mankiller was not the first woman to succeed in modern tribal politics. Two of the most important early trailblazers in that arena were Annie Dodge Wauneka (1910–1997) and Betty Mae Tiger Jumper (1923–).

The daughter of Navajo leader Henry Chee Dodge, Annie Dodge Wauneka dedicated her life to improving the living conditions and health care available to poor tribe members. Wauneka's devotion to her people won her a position on the Navajo Tribal Council in 1951. The first woman to serve on the council, she was reelected to this office twice. After retiring from the council, Wauneka worked tirelessly to promote both Western medicine and traditional healing methods to help the Navajos deal with epidemic disease and other health problems. In 1963 Wauneka became the first American Indian to receive the Presidential Medal of Freedom, the highest honor the U.S. government can bestow on a civilian.

A member of the Seminole Tribe of Florida, Betty Mae Tiger Jumper was a nurse before she entered politics. In 1957, when the Seminoles held their first modern election, Jumper took a seat on the Seminole Tribal Council. Ten years later, she was elected tribal chief—the first Indian woman of any tribe to hold such a high position. After completing her four-year term, Jumper was the publisher of a tribal newspaper for many years. She continues to lecture on Seminole history and culture and has written several books, including her autobiography, *A Seminole Legend: The Life of Betty Mae Tiger Jumper* (2001).

Navajo politician Annie Dodge Wauneka shows off a doll wearing nineteenth-century Navajo clothing.

be achieved was if Mankiller continued to work toward them as principal chief.

THE 1987 ELECTION

In the 1987 election, Mankiller faced three opponents: Dave Whitekiller, Perry Wheeler, and William McKee. As she ran against three men, Mankiller's gender again became a campaign issue. Whitekiller particularly disapproved of women in leadership roles. He claimed the Cherokees had lost the respect of other tribes during the years that Mankiller served as chief. Whitekiller also criticized Mankiller for not using her husband's name. He unsuccessfully tried to persuade the tribal election committee to list her surname as Soap on the ballot.

Mankiller's most formidable challenger was Perry Wheeler. A former deputy chief, Wheeler had run a strong campaign for principal chief against Swimmer in 1983. Wheeler criticized Mankiller for lacking business and managerial experience. Making fun of her time in San Francisco, he implied that she was part of what he called the "hippie craze" of the 1960s and 1970s.

Mankiller vowed to run a "positive forward-thinking campaign." She tried to ignore what her opponents were saying and concentrated on spreading a hopeful message. With John Ketcher as her running mate, she emphasized her desire to improve the Cherokees' housing, health care, and educational facilities.

In June the Cherokees went to the polls. Mankiller and Ketcher received the most votes in their respective races. Neither, however, received enough to avoid a runoff. In the runoff election, Mankiller was up against Wheeler, and Ketcher ran against Barbara Starr-Scott, Wheeler's choice for deputy chief.

With her husband Charlie by her side, Mankiller started campaigning hard. She knew she had to reach as many voters as possible in the weeks before the runoff. As the election date neared, however, Mankiller became extremely ill. She was admitted into a hospital in Tulsa with a severe kidney infection. It had resulted from polycystic kidney disease, which Mankiller had inherited from her father. Her doctors had difficulty treating the infection, and Mankiller suffered permanent kidney damage.

While she was in the hospital, Wheeler started a telephone campaign. His callers told the Cherokees not to waste their vote on Mankiller because she was going to die. The maneuver forced Mankiller to hold a press conference from her hospital bed just to assure her supporters that she was still very much alive.

Mankiller survived not only her latest health crisis, but also her latest political challenge. Just before midnight on the night of the election, Wheeler conceded. Mankiller had won the runoff.

In one sense, little had changed for Mankiller. She was still principal chief, just as she had been before the 1987 campaign began. But after the election, Mankiller felt different about her position. She was no longer principal chief by chance. She was now the leader of the Cherokees because they had chosen her to lead them.

CHAPTER SEVEN

The Chief
of a Nation

A FTER THE 1987 ELECTION, MANKILLER felt more relaxed in her role as principal chief. During her first two years in her job, she was always a little tense, always afraid of making a mistake. She worried that her mistakes would not only reflect badly on her, but also bring into question other women's ability to lead. As she explained,

> **I would think to myself that if I did not make it to this meeting or to that session, it would reflect poorly on all women. I felt that not only my credibility but also the credibility of any woman who might follow me was on the line.**

The election results emboldened Mankiller. The Cherokee voters had spoken, and with their votes the majority had backed Mankiller's plans for the Cherokee Nation. With this mandate, Mankiller was more determined than ever to improve the lives of her people.

Wilma Mankiller poses in front of the tribal emblem at Cherokee Nation Headquarters in Oklahoma.

During the late 1980s and early 1990s, Mankiller oversaw a wide variety of projects for the Cherokee Nation. Her administration worked to improve everything from the sewer and road systems to day care and foster care programs. Mankiller was particularly interested in health care. While she was chief, several new health clinics were constructed to serve Cherokees in smaller communities.

Education was another priority. Under Mankiller's administration, the Cherokee Nation improved its facilities for Head Start, an educational program for preschoolers run by the federal government. Mankiller also worked to improve the management of Sequoyah High School in Tahlequah. Mankiller's government increased the number of college scholarships available to Cherokee students and expanded bilingual programs that helped teach the Cherokee language to both children and adults.

One of Mankiller's biggest goals was saving the Talking Leaves Jobs Corps Center. Established in 1978, this center provided job training for young Cherokees and other youths in the region. It had been housed in a dormitory leased to the Cherokees by Northeastern State University in Tahlequah. The university needed more space, however, so it refused to renew the Cherokees' lease, which was due to expire in November 1987.

Mankiller asked the tribal council for help in solving the problem. She proposed that they close a struggling hotel and restaurant run by the Cherokee Nation and use the buildings for the job center instead. The council declined her request. Mankiller refused to back down. She said she would take the issue to the Cherokees and launch an "all-out political war" if she had to. The council finally relented. Mankiller counts saving the job center as one of her greatest accomplishments as chief.

ATTRACTING BUSINESS

Mankiller had considerable success in the areas of health care, housing, and education. She often struggled in her efforts in economic development, however. She tried to attract businesses to the Cherokee Nation, but reaching that goal was far from easy. It was especially difficult in rural areas, where there were few educated workers and inadequate roads.

Mankiller had hoped that tribal businesses could bring in enough money to help fund health care improvements. When that failed to be the case, she made a hard decision. She decided the Cherokee government should run bingo parlors in order to raise revenue. In the United States, many Indian tribes operate bingo parlors and casinos. Legally, these businesses are not subject to state laws that forbid gambling operations within state borders. With little competition, these tribal gambling businesses are often very profitable.

Mankiller was uncomfortable with promoting gambling within the Cherokee Nation. But in the end, she decided that funding health care was more important. She later recalled that the decision to advocate bingo parlors gave her "a lot of mixed feelings." According to Mankiller, "it was the only thing I ever remember doing [while working for the Cherokee Nation] that I came home and cried about." By the end of her tenure as chief, the Cherokees were operating three bingo parlors. They were the most profitable of all the tribe's businesses.

Another landmark in Mankiller's political career was signing a self-governance compact, or agreement, between the Cherokee Nation and the U.S. government in 1990. For decades, Indian groups had worked hard for more say in programs funded and administered by the Bureau of Indian Affairs. Mankiller, along with four other tribal leaders, negotiated the compact, which gave their tribes more input than ever before in how to spend money for health care, education, and other tribal services. Mankiller declared that the compact was

> **a significant step toward the Cherokee Nation once again assuming control over our own resources.**

FIGHTING FOR HER LIFE

When Mankiller signed the compact, she was recovering from still another health crisis. In late 1989, Mankiller's kidney problems had progressed dangerously. She was close to total kidney failure. Mankiller needed a kidney transplant, but first she had to find a kidney donor. Weaker by the minute, she asked family members if they were willing to give her a kidney. Her sister Frances seemed like the best candidate. But after a battery of tests, doctors determined that Frances's overall health was not sound enough to put her through the difficult and painful surgery.

Mankiller's husband then called Wilma's older brother, Don. Don had always had an intense fear of hospitals. Even so, he agreed to be tested and was found to be a perfect match. Don had surgery to remove his kidney, which then was transplanted into his sister's body.

The kidney transplant was a great success. Mankiller felt pangs of guilt, however, as she watched Don suffer through his excruciating recovery. In her autobiography she acknowledges the sacrifice he made for her. Its dedication reads,

> **to my brother Louis Donald Mankiller, who gave up much of his youth to feed and clothe his siblings. Then in 1990, he donated a kidney to me, enabling me to continue with my life and work in good health."**

ANOTHER ELECTION

By early 1991 Mankiller was healthy enough to launch her second campaign for principal chief. This time around she was a seasoned candidate, well schooled in how ugly political races could get. Mankiller was prepared to throw all her energy and attention into a difficult campaign. As she said, "If one sleeps during this period, one is liable to lose the entire election."

The 1991 campaign proved to be the smoothest of her career. After six years as chief, Mankiller could run on a solid record of achievement. She touted her work in health care, education, and Cherokee self-government. Her critics still claimed she had not done enough to develop the Cherokee economy, but most Cherokees were satisfied by what she had achieved in office. As one tribe member explained, "[S]he'd done everything she promised the people. . . . She's probably been the most aggressive chief we've ever had."

THE UNITED KEETOOWAH BAND

In the 1830s the Cherokees lost control of their homeland in the Southeast. After that, there were two branches of the Cherokee tribe. They eventually became known as the Cherokee Nation and the Eastern Band of Cherokee Indians.

In 1950 the United States recognized a third Cherokee tribe. It is known as the United Keetoowah Band (UKB) of Cherokee Indians. In recent years, the relationship between the Cherokee Nation and the UKB has been strained. During the administration of Wilma Mankiller, the two groups clashed when the Cherokee Nation tried to force smoke shops run by UKB members to pay state taxes in compliance with an agreement between the Cherokee Nation and the State of Oklahoma. The disputes between the UKB and the Cherokee Nation are ongoing.

All the attention Mankiller received from the press also persuaded many people that she was a good choice as chief. With Mankiller in charge, the Cherokees and their concerns had received more national press coverage than ever before.

Mankiller's strength as a candidate scared off all prominent rivals. She ran against two men—William K. Dew and Art Nave—but neither was well known in political circles. When the Cherokees went to the polls, Mankiller, for the first time, had enough votes to avoid a runoff. In fact, she won in a landslide. Mankiller received an astounding 82 percent of the votes—a testament to her strong support across the Cherokee Nation.

WHO IS A CHEROKEE?

During her second term, Mankiller courted controversy because of her efforts to keep non-Cherokees from using the Cherokee name. The U.S. government legally recognizes only three groups of Cherokees—the Cherokee Nation of Oklahoma, the United Keetoowah Band of Cherokee Indians (located in Oklahoma), and the Eastern Band of Cherokee Indians (located in North Carolina). Federal recognition entitles these tribes to U.S. government funds and services detailed in past treaties and agreements.

Many Americans who do not belong to these groups claim Cherokee ancestry. In the 2000 census, 729,533 U.S. citizens identified themselves as at least part Cherokee—a number far higher than the population of the three federally recognized Cherokee groups. Thus, hundreds of thousands of Americans call themselves Cherokee even though they are not enrolled members of a Cherokee tribe. Some of these people have Cherokee ancestry, but they do not have the documentation of their background needed to satisfy the requirements for tribal enrollment. But the claims of many would-be Cherokees are even less substantial. Some have heard old—and likely untrue—family stories about Cherokee relatives. Others simply make up Cherokee bloodlines. They think calling themselves Cherokees makes them seem more interesting or exotic.

Mankiller held no grudge against individuals who, with no real proof, said they were part Cherokee. But she was angry about groups of people who called themselves Cherokees in hopes of getting money from the federal government. While she was chief, Mankiller sent a list of such groups to state and federal officials, along with warnings that their members were not part of an actual Cherokee tribe.

TELLING HER OWN STORY

Toward the end of her tenure as principal chief, Mankiller, with co-author Michael Wallis, penned her autobiography. Titled *Mankiller: A Chief and Her People* (1993), it intertwines the story of her life with a history of the Cherokees. A critical and popular success, the book was a national best seller. As the quotations below show, much of the book's appeal comes from Mankiller's ability to translate her own experiences into inspirational lessons readers can apply to their own lives.

On coping with illness and injury: "When the going got especially difficult, I allowed my mind to slip away to the past. Going back in time and space can sometimes help remedy a person's troubles" (page 77).

On refusing to give up on a goal: "I think my father's tenacity is a characteristic I inherited. Once I set my mind to do something, I never give up. I was raised in a household where no one ever said to me, 'You can't do this because you're a woman, Indian, or poor.' No one told me there were limitations. Of course, I would not have listened to them if they had tried" (page 112).

On coming to terms with death: "[My near-fatal car] accident changed my life. I had experienced death, felt its presence, touched it, and then let it go. It was a very spiritual thing, a rare natural gift" (page 226).

On learning lessons from adversity: "[Becoming principal chief of the Cherokees never] would have happened if it had not been for the ordeals I had survived in the first place. After that, I realized I could survive anything. I had faced adversity and turned it into a positive experience—a better path. I had found the way to be of good mind" (page 229).

On building a strong marital relationship: "From the onset, [my relationship with my husband] was solid as a rock. It all stemmed from a deep respect. It is the strongest love I have ever known. We genuinely like each other. We never seem to get bored, and I think we continue to bring out each other's strengths" (page 237).

On encouraging women to become leaders: "I have attained a leadership position because I am willing to take risks. . . . Friends describe me as someone who likes to dance along the edge of the roof. I try to encourage young women to be willing to take risks, to stand up for the things they believe in, and to step up and accept the challenge of serving in leadership roles" (page 250).

Mankiller also tried to block several groups trying to get state recognition as tribes—a stepping-stone to federal recognition. In 1993, when the state legislature of Georgia voted to recognize three American-Indian tribes, Mankiller wrote an angry letter to Georgia governor Zell Miller and urged him to veto the bill: "I was shocked and dismayed to learn that the Georgia legislature passed a law recognizing three 'Indian tribes,' two of them purportedly Cherokee! . . . Our concern deals with states creating Indian tribes without specific recognition criteria. . . . The United States has a complex set of criteria. . . . Anyone even minimally versed in Indian legal or political affairs is aware that federal recognition of an Indian tribe is a very serious matter." Despite her efforts, Georgia officially recognized the Cherokee Indians of Georgia and the Georgia Tribe of Eastern Cherokees.

MANKILLER IN NATIONAL POLITICS

Throughout her three terms in office, Mankiller was not just a leading voice in tribal politics. She was also an important politician on the national stage. Because of the media's glowing coverage of Mankiller, she was the most famous American-Indian leader in the country. Mankiller used this notoriety not only to promote the welfare of the Cherokees, but also to draw attention to issues of importance to all Indian tribes. She testified before Congress to discuss the need for better health care, housing, and educational opportunities for Indian peoples.

Mankiller met with three U.S. presidents while chief of the Cherokee Nation. During her first four years in office, Republican Ronald Reagan was president. A staunch Democrat, Mankiller disagreed with nearly all of Reagan's policies. She and many other Indian leaders were also angry about a controversial statement Reagan made about the historical relationship between the U.S. government and Indian peoples. In May 1988, while visiting the Union of Soviet Socialist Republics (USSR), a young journalist asked Reagan about America's past suppression of racial minorities. The president blithely answered that the United States should never have "humored" Indian tribes by allowing them to "live a primitive lifestyle."

In the final weeks of his presidency, Reagan met with sixteen American-Indian leaders. Mankiller and two others had been chosen as the group's spokespeople. It was Mankiller's first visit to the White House. In her own words, she was "overwhelmed" by the

Mankiller sits next to President Ronald Reagan during a meeting of tribal leaders held at the White House in 1988.

"enormous responsibility to have to speak for all of the tribes of the United States." The meeting was a disappointment. Mankiller felt the president showed little interest in the issues that the tribal leaders raised.

Mankiller was more impressed by President George H. W. Bush. Although she opposed Bush's cuts to social programs funded by the federal government, she thought his administration took Indian policy seriously. Mankiller felt Bush's advisers listened to Indian leaders and respected Indian sovereignty enough to deal with tribes in a government-to-government relationship.

Mankiller was even more enthusiastic about the presidency of Bill Clinton. She endorsed his candidacy and urged other Indian leaders to support him, largely because of his record on environmental issues. After Clinton was elected, he invited Mankiller to join with leaders in American business and industry at a highly publicized economic conference in Little Rock, Arkansas, in December 1992.

During Clinton's presidency, Mankiller met with the U.S. attorney general and proposed that the administration organize a meeting of all tribal leaders in Washington. Clinton approved Mankiller's idea and invited the leaders of the 547 federally recognized tribes to a summit to discuss the most pressing Indian issues, from tribal gaming to the management of reservation resources to law enforcement in Indian communities. More than 320 Indian leaders were able to attend the forum, which was held on April 29, 1994. It was biggest gathering of tribal leaders ever assembled.

Clinton asked Mankiller to moderate the event. For two hours, she introduced a selection of tribal leaders, who made presentations before the president, vice president, and all the members of Clinton's cabinet. It was then the president's turn to speak. At the podium he marked the historical occasion with words of hope and reconciliation: "Of course, as you well know, our history has not always been a proud one. But our future can be, and that is up to us. Together we can open the greatest era of cooperation, understanding, and respect among our people ever."

Mankiller and First Lady Hillary Rodham Clinton discussing Indian health care issues with U.S. senators in 1993. Mankiller supported Clinton's campaign for the presidency in 2008.

CHAPTER EIGHT

JOHN ROSS
1790 – 1866
PRINCIPAL CHIEF
OF THE
CHEROKEE NATION
1828 – 1866

SEAL OF THE CHEROKEE NATION
SEPT. 6, 1839

Mankiller's Legacy

I N THE SPRING OF 1995, MANKILLER'S SECOND full term as principal chief was coming to an end. With that in mind, she called together hundreds of employees of the Cherokee Nation and made a surprise announcement: she would not be a candidate in the upcoming election.

"I've been here seventeen years," Mankiller said. "I've grown up and become a grandmother. I've met with three presidents, lobbied Congress for everything from job corps to Head Start and been given more awards and honors than any one person deserves." But after ten years as principal chief, she felt it was time to move on.

Many people at first assumed Mankiller was ending her political career because of health problems, but she denied that was the case: "I'm actually in good health now and I want to keep it that way," Mankiller explained.

A CRISIS IN CHEROKEE POLITICS

After Wilma Mankiller announced that she would not run for reelection, a reporter asked her whom she wanted to succeed her as chief. She said,

> It's up to [the Cherokees] to decide, not me. I just hope we don't see the politics of hate in 1995 that we saw in the previous election.

Wilma Mankiller poses beside a memorial of an earlier principal chief of the Cherokee Nation, John Ross.

The 1995 election turned out to be even more contentious than those Mankiller ran in. It also ushered in one of the most tumultuous periods in modern Cherokee politics.

During the campaign, Mankiller endorsed George Bearpaw, the nation's executive director for tribal operations. When the votes were counted, Bearpaw won, but not by a high enough margin to avoid a runoff against the second-place candidate, Joe Byrd. Before the runoff election, however, it came out that Bearpaw had pled guilty to an assault charge twenty years earlier. The Cherokee Judicial Appeals Tribunal said that Bearpaw was disqualified from running for office. Unopposed in the runoff, Joe Byrd became the new principal chief.

Two years into Byrd's term, the tribal police began investigating a possible misuse of tribal funds by Byrd. When fifteen marshals arrived to search his office, Byrd fired them. The tribal court then issued a warrant for the principal chief's arrest. He punished the court's three justices by persuading the tribal council to impeach them.

The Cherokee government was in a stage of chaos. Its three branches were all warring for power. Agents from the Bureau of Indian Affairs had to be called in to keep the peace. Mankiller said the situation was "heartbreaking":

"It's tragic to watch the unraveling of a constitutional government, and that is what we're seeing here."

In 1999, Byrd lost his reelection bid to a lawyer named Chad Smith. BIA agents remained in the Cherokee Nation for four years after the new principal chief took office. Smith was reelected in 2003 and 2007.

A TEACHER, A SPEAKER, AND A WRITER

After leaving office, Mankiller decided to accept an invitation to teach at Yale University in New Haven, Connecticut. She was awarded a Chubb Fellowship, which brings to the school politicians, activists, and artists involved in public service. Mankiller later served as a visiting professor at Dartmouth College in New Hampshire and at the University of Oregon.

While she enjoyed the academic world, Mankiller had little desire to take a permanent university post. As she once explained about her time at Dartmouth, "[T]he intellectual stimulation was incredible. But for me, it was empty. You know, it was, sure, I read all these great books. It was great to sit down to have dinner with the president of an Ivy League College or something, but I wanted to be home." Home continued to be in Mankiller Flats. She lived there with her husband Charlie. Her daughter Gina lives close by.

In addition to teaching, Mankiller enjoyed presenting lectures around the world. Her speeches often focused on the challenges that American Indians and women face in the twenty-first century. Mankiller also served on the boards of trustees of several important nonprofit groups, including the Ford Foundation and the Ms. Foundation for Women. More recently, Mankiller was appointed to the board of the Freedom Forum, which operates the Newseum. This museum opened in Washington, D.C., in 2008. Its exhibits display the history of journalism and promote freedom of the press.

Mankiller also pursued a career as an author. While still serving as principal chief, Mankiller wrote her autobiography, *Mankiller: A Chief and Her People* (1993), with co-author Michael Wallis. For her second book, Mankiller chose an ambitious reference work titled *The Reader's Companion to U.S. Women's History*

(1998). With four other co-editors, Mankiller compiled some four hundred articles about the experiences and contributions of American women.

Again serving as editor, Mankiller compiled *Every Day Is a Good Day: Reflections by Contemporary Indigenous Women*, which was published in 2004. The book contains profiles of nineteen American-Indian women who have distinguished themselves as activists, artists, educators, and other professionals. Each story is introduced by an essay written by Mankiller. According to a review in *Booklist*, the book offers "[p]rofound yet simple words from strong women working hard to perpetuate their culture, and who have a lot to share, and who need to be heard."

Mankiller also wrote numerous articles and essays. For instance, she penned the introduction to *Reflections on American Indian History: Honoring the Past, Building a Future* (2008). This book of scholarly articles grew out of the Wilma Mankiller Symposium on American History, a meeting of historians that was named in her honor.

A NATIONAL FIGURE

Mankiller received a host of awards for her work. She held more than a dozen honorary doctoral degrees from such institutions such as Mills College, Yale University, Smith College, and the University of Oklahoma. She also received the John W. Gardner Leadership Award and was inducted into the National Women's Hall of Fame. On January 15, 1998, Mankiller received her most prestigious honor. President Bill Clinton awarded her with the Presidential Medal of Freedom, the highest honor that the U.S. government can give a civilian citizen. Clinton hailed Mankiller "not only as the guardian of the centuries-old

In 1998 President Bill Clinton presented Mankiller with the Presidential Medal of Freedom during a White House ceremony.

Cherokee heritage but a revered leader who built a brighter and healthier future for her nation."

Although Mankiller retired from Cherokee politics in 1995, she remained an important voice on the national political stage. During the 2008 presidential campaign, she served as a national campaign co-chair for Democratic candidate Hillary Rodham Clinton. Clinton expressed her appreciation for Mankiller's endorsement by stating, "I am honored and humbled to have the support of a deeply respected woman who knows what it takes to lead a nation."

After Clinton's defeat in the Democratic primary, Mankiller threw her support to Barack Obama. In an editorial published in *Indian Country Today*, Mankiller said that Obama not only was the best candidate on the issues she cared most about—"tribal sovereignty, foreign policy and health"—but also had helped restore her faith in the political process:

As a Native woman, it is tough not to feel distrustful of and cynical toward most politicians. But on the crest of this election season, unlike any prior, I feel buoyed. I feel energized, engaged and excited. I feel something new: hope.

IN SERVICE TO THE CHEROKEES

Through her activism, speaking, and writing, Mankiller continued to influence American thought and politics. During her long career in the public eye, however, she had already had a great impact in several arenas. Most obviously, through her years in public service, she had a hand in transforming the Cherokee Nation.

Mankiller's early work on community development not only revitalized the town of Bell, but also provided the Cherokees with a model for rebuilding other ailing communities. While chief, Mankiller initiated a series of new development projects, using the same self-help approach she had employed in Bell.

Mankiller also made strides in improving education and health care. Willing to battle a resistant tribal council, she managed to find a new home for the Talking Leaves Job Corps Center. The center now offers job training to about 270 young people each year. Acknowledging her devotion to improving tribe members' access to basic health care, the Cherokees named the Wilma Mankiller Health Clinic in Stilwell, Oklahoma, in her honor.

Mankiller also used her fame to bring attention to issues affecting the Cherokees. As chief, she forged important political alliances in Washington, D.C., which helped her secure federal funding for important projects. Through interviews and lectures, Mankiller taught the public about the problems facing Indian peoples today. She was especially eager to discuss the important role that tribal governments play in the lives of Indian peoples and to promote respect for tribal sovereignty.

Mankiller also saw public appearances as an opportunity to teach non-Indians about Indian history and culture. For instance, in 2007, Mankiller was asked to speak during the festivities surrounding the centennial celebration of Oklahoma statehood. At first, she was hesitant to participate. Mankiller saw the event as nothing to celebrate, because the western Cherokees lost a great deal of their territory during the years when Oklahoma prepared to join the Union. Mankiller reconsidered when she realized it was a good chance to share her knowledge about the Cherokees and other peoples. As she explained at the time, "People don't like to be preached to. If you want them to learn about tribal history and tribal culture and tribal values, you need to kind of extend a hand and say, 'You know, let's sit down for a while and talk.' I see this centennial lecture as an opportunity to do that."

In many lectures, Mankiller tried to educate her audience about contemporary Indians. She worked to dismantle outdated stereotypes about Indian life by challenging non-Indians "to not just see us as a people that dances and makes nice baskets." At the same time, she encouraged her listeners to see beyond the superficial similarities between the day-to-day lives of Indians and those of other Americans:

> **A lot of Americans think that because we dress like people around us, we drive similar cars, we live in similar houses, we think the same way. I would contend we not only think about different things, but we think about them in a different way.**

Mankiller also stressed that "ancient tribal cultures have important lessons to teach the rest of the world about the interconnectedness of all living things and the simple fact that our existence is dependent upon the natural world we are rapidly destroying. The traditional value systems that have sustained us throughout the past five hundred years of trauma are those value systems that will bolster us and help us enter the twenty-first century on our own terms."

The high-profile and positive publicity Mankiller received over the years has affected many Indian people on a deeply personal level. Indians who have been insulted and degraded because of their ancestry have reveled in her success. Especially after the publication of her autobiography, Mankiller received bags of fan letters from Indians who felt inspired by her story. Some thanked her for helping make them proud of being an Indian. Many other fans—both Indian and non-Indian—wrote to say that reading her story made them want to learn about Indian history and culture.

INSPIRING OTHERS TO ACT

Mankiller's autobiography also struck a chord with people suffering from serious illnesses and disabilities. Many were moved by the story of her long recovery from her car accident and her battle with kidney disease. After leaving office, Mankiller's reputation as a survivor only grew with publicity surrounding other severe health scares. In 1996 she was diagnosed with lymphoma, but she was treated successfully with chemotherapy. Two years later, Mankiller had a second kidney transplant. More recently, Mankiller battled both breast and colon cancer. In March 2010 her husband announced that she had also been diagnosed with advanced pancreatic cancer. Throughout her struggles, Mankiller had inspired others battling similar illnesses by remaining upbeat and active.

Sadly, on April 6, 2010, Mankiller finally succumbed to pancreatic cancer at the age of sixty-four. Weeks before her death, her husband issued a press release, in which she assured her friends and admirers that she was prepared for the end of her life. She said she felt blessed by the full life she had led and the many extraordinary experiences she had had.

In addition to inspiring the ill and disabled, Mankiller also became a role model for young women. Although she was not the first Indian woman to carve out a career in tribal politics, she was unique in the amount of attention she received. Publicity about Mankiller's achievements helped inspire American-Indian women across the country to get involved in the politics of their tribes.

Mankiller also inspired non-Indian women. Throughout her political career, Mankiller encouraged women from all backgrounds to take on leadership roles in their communities and in government.

Mankiller's success certainly had special significance for American Indians and women, who all too often have been shut out of leadership roles in the past. But her story can appeal to anyone who has ever felt beaten down by circumstance and overwhelmed by a sense of powerlessness over his or her life. Mankiller faced extraordinary challenges—from extreme poverty to a difficult marriage to life-threatening diseases—but instead of giving in to despair, she cultivated a positive attitude, or what she called "a Cherokee approach" to life.

Just as inspiring is Mankiller's lifelong willingness to get involved and to do whatever she felt needed doing. It is exactly this quality that she sought to foster in others. In a 2000 interview published in *Tulsa World*, she spoke of her frustration with people who say,

> **'[S]omebody needs to do something about that' or 'I hope they're going to do something about this.' Who are 'they'? Where is the 'somebody' who's supposed to do something about it?**

Mankiller asked. Providing her own answer, she said,

> **The truth is, there are no great saviors. There are no great heroes that are going to come in to solve all of these problems.**

Mankiller is certainly a hero to many. But perhaps her greatest legacy is this simple message: instead of looking around for heroes to reshape what is wrong in the world, we should strive to find the hero in ourselves, that strong inner core that will fight for change no matter what. As Mankiller once said,

> **We're going to have to do it.
> People like you and people like me:
> people who are willing to step up and lead.**

FEMALE TRIBAL LEADERS

In 1985 Wilma Mankiller's inauguration as the first female chief of the Cherokee Nation became international news. Since that time, many other Indian women have followed in her footsteps by becoming the first women to lead their tribes. The women profiled below are just a few of these historic firsts.

JOYCE DUGAN

The superintendent of schools for the Eastern Band of Cherokee Indians, Joyce Dugan beat out nine other candidates to become the tribe's chief in 1995. In this position, she modernized the structure of the tribal government and worked to improve health care and to set environmental standards on the tribe's reservation.

VIVIAN JUAN-SAUNDERS

Vivian Juan-Saunders was elected chairperson of the Tohono O'odham Nation in 2003. During her tenure, she tried to attract industry to the tribe's reservation and to improve the housing available for tribe members.

CECILIA FIRE THUNDER

A former nurse, Cecilia Fire Thunder was elected president of the Oglala Sioux Tribe of South Dakota in 2004. Her brief time in office was fraught with controversy. Fire Thunder angered her tribal council when, as South Dakota was considering a statewide abortion ban, she announced her intention to establish a Planned Parenthood clinic on tribal land. The council impeached Fire Thunder in 2006.

ERMA J. VIZENOR

For many years, Erma J. Vizenor fought corruption in the government of the White Earth Band of the Chippewa of Minnesota. A former teacher, she joined the tribal council in 1996 and was elected tribal chairperson in 2004. Vizenor has since worked to improve economic opportunities, education, and health care on the White Earth Indian Reservation. She was reelected in 2008 with 66 percent of the vote.

GLENNA J. WALLACE

In 2006 Glenna J. Wallace left her job as a communications instructor at Crowder College in Neosho, Missouri, to become the chief of the Eastern Shawnee Tribe. She has worked to promote the tribe's cultural heritage and establish more tribally owned casinos and other businesses.

TIMELINE

1945 — Born in Mankiller Flats in northeastern Oklahoma

1956 — Family moves to San Francisco, California, as part of the Bureau of Indian Affairs relocation program

1963 — Marries Hugo Olaya

1969–1971 — Lends behind-the-scenes support to the nineteen-month occupation of Alcatraz Island by the Indians of All Tribes

1974 — Divorces Hugo Olaya

1977 — Returns to Oklahoma with daughters Gina and Felicia; begins working for the Cherokee Nation as an economic stimulus coordinator

1979 — Becomes a community development specialist for the Cherokee Nation; is nearly killed in an automobile accident

1980 — Diagnosed and treated for myasthenia gravis, a form of muscular dystrophy

1983 — Elected deputy chief of the Cherokee Nation of Oklahoma

1985 — Becomes the first female principal chief of the western Cherokees after the resignation of Ross Swimmer

1986 — Marries Charlie Soap

1987	Becomes the first elected female principal chief of the Cherokee Nation of Oklahoma; is named *Ms.* magazine Woman of the Year
1990	Undergoes a lifesaving kidney transplant; signs self-governance compact between the Cherokee Nation and the United States
1991	Elected to a third term as principal chief, with more than 82 percent of the vote
1993	Publishes autobiography, *Mankiller: A Chief and Her People*
1994	Moderates historic meeting between President Bill Clinton and the leaders of federally recognized American-Indian tribes
1995	Declines to run for reelection and retires from political life; receives a Chubb Fellowship from Yale University
1996	Serves as a Montgomery Fellow at Dartmouth College
1998	Awarded the Presidential Medal of Freedom by President Bill Clinton; has second kidney transplant
2004	*Every Day Is a Good Day*, a collection of profiles of American-Indian women, is published
2005	Serves as the Morse Chair Professor of Law and Politics at the University of Oregon
2008	Becomes a national campaign cochair for presidential candidate Hillary Rodham Clinton; endorses Barack Obama in the general election
2010	Dies of pancreatic cancer at her home near Tahlequah, Oklahoma

SOURCE NOTES

Boxed quotes unless otherwise noted

CHAPTER 1

p. 5, par. 1, Wilma Mankiller and Michael Wallis, *Mankiller: A Chief and Her People* (New York: St. Martin's Press, 1993), p. 245.

p. 5, Ibid.

p. 8, Ibid., p. 35.

p. 12, par. 1, Ibid., p. 33.

p. 13, par. 1, Ibid., p. 38.

p. 14, Ibid., p. 37.

p. 14, par. 4, Ibid., p. 40.

p. 15, par. 1, Ibid., p. 41.

CHAPTER 2

p. 17, par. 3, Sarah Eppler Janda, *Beloved Women: The Political Lives of LaDonna Harris and Wilma Mankiller* (DeKalb: Northern Illinois University Press, 2007), p. 81.

p. 20, par. 1, Mankiller and Wallis, p. 70.

p. 20, par. 3, Wilma Mankiller, interview, "Campfire Stories with George Catlin," Smithsonian American Art Museum, http://americanart2.si.edu/collections/exhibits/catlinclassroom/interviews/al-mankiller.html (accessed February 7, 2009).

p. 20, par. 2, Mankiller and Wallis, p. 71.

p. 21, par. 2, Ibid., p. 73.

p. 21, par. 2, Ibid., p. 76.

p. 23, Ibid., p. 103.

p. 23, par. 4, Ibid., p. 106.

p. 25, par. 1, Ibid., p. 108.

p. 25, Ibid., p. 110.

p. 25, R. David Edmunds, ed., *The New Warriors* (Lincoln: University of Nebraska Press, 2001), p. 212.

CHAPTER 3

p. 29, par. 1, Mankiller and Wallis, p. 144.

p. 29, par. 2, Ibid., p. 145.

p. 29, par. 4, Ibid., p. 146.

p. 30, par. 1, Ibid., p. 147.

p. 30, par. 3, Ibid., p. 150.

p. 30, Sam Howe Verhovek, "At Work With: Chief Wilma Mankiller; The Name's the Most and Least of Her," *New York Times*, November 4, 1993.

p. 33, Mankiller and Wallis, p. 157.

p. 33, par. Ibid., p. 159.

p. 38, par. 1, Ibid., p. 193.

p. 38, Ibid., p. 192.

p. 38, par. 2, Ibid., p. 197.

p. 39, par. 1, Ibid., p. 201.

p. 39, par. 2, Ibid., p. 202.

p. 39, Ibid., p. 203.

p. 40, Ibid.

CHAPTER 4

p. 43, Ibid., p. 205.

p. 43, par. 2, Ibid., p. 215.

p. 45, Ibid., p. 217.

p. 45, Ibid.

p. 46, Edmunds, p. 213.

p. 47, Mankiller and Wallis, p. 222.

p. 47, par. 3, Ibid., p. 223.

p. 47, Ibid.

p. 48, Ibid., p. 224.

p. 48, Ibid., p. 226.

p. 49, par. 1, Ibid.

p. 49, par. 3, Ibid., p. 227.

p. 49, par. 5, Edmunds, p. 214.

CHAPTER 5

p. 53, Janda, p. 79.

p. 54, par. 3, Edmunds, p. 215.

p. 55, par. 1, Mankiller and Wallis, p. 240.

p. 55, Ibid.

p. 59, Ibid.

p. 59, par. 3, Ibid., p. 241.

p. 59, Ibid.

p. 60, Janda, p. 95.

p. 61, Mankiller and Wallis, p. 241.

p. 62, par. 4, Janda, p. 76.

p. 63, Edmunds, p. 217.

CHAPTER 6

p. 65, Janda, p. 118.

p. 66, par. 4, Ibid., p. 98.

p. 67, par. 3, Mankiller and Wallis, p. 3.

p. 69, par. 4, Ibid., p. 247.

p. 72, par. 3, Ibid., p. 249.

p. 72, par. 4, Ibid., p. 247.

CHAPTER 7

p. 75, Ibid., p. 251.

p. 77, par. 1, Edmunds, p. 220.

p. 77, par. 4, Ibid., p. 222.

p. 78, Ibid., pp. 224-25.

p. 79, Mankiller and Wallis, p. v.

p. 79, par. 2, Janda, p. 119.

p. 79, par. 3, Edmunds, p. 224.

p. 84, par. 1, Janda, p. 120.

p. 85, par. 1, Liz Sonneborn, *Chronology of American Indian History, Updated Edition* (New York: Facts On File, 2007), p. 357.

p. 86, par. 1, Edmunds, p. 223.

p. 87, par. 1, Government Printing Office's Federal Digital System,

Compilation of Presidential Documents (1993 to Present), http://fdsys.
gpo.gov/fdsys/pkg/WCPD-1994-05-09/pdf/WCPD-1994-05-09-
Pg941.pdf (accessed February, 20, 2009).

CHAPTER 8

p. 89, par. 2, Janda, p. 133.

p. 89, par. 3, Edmunds, p. 227.

p. 89, Edmunds, p. 228.

p. 90, Verhovek, p. 1.

p. 91, par. 2, Mankiller, interview, "Campfire Stories with George Catlin."

p. 92, par. 2, Reviews of *Every Day is a Good Day*, Amazon.com, www.
amazon.com/Every-Day-Good-Reflections-Contemporary/
dp/1555915167/ref=sr_1_1?ie=UTF8&s=books&qid=1237065289&
sr=1-1 (accessed February 14, 2009).

p. 92, par. 4, Edmunds, p. 229.

p. 94, par. 2, "Former Cherokee Nation Principal Chief Wilma Mankiller
Endorses Hillary Clinton," HillaryClinton.com, http://townhall.
hillaryclinton.com/news/release/view/?id=5723 (accessed February
21, 2009).

p. 94, par. 3, "Mankiller: Obama an Advocate for Indian Country,"
Indian Country Today, August 22, 2008, www.indianz.com/
News/2008/010463.asp (accessed March 2, 2009).

p. 94, Ibid.

p. 96, par. 1, Judy Gibbs Robinson, "Mankiller Opens Up Dialogue:
Centennial Offers a Chance to See New Perspectives, Former Cherokee
Chief Says," *Daily Oklahoman*, February 23, 2007, www.newsok.com/
article/3017189 (accessed March 1, 2009).

p. 96, par. 2, Janda, p. 130.

p. 96, Robinson.

p. 97, Ibid.

p. 98, par. 3, Edmunds, p. 214.

p. 98, Becky Tiernan, "Mankiller Encourages Action," *Tulsa World*, March 9,
2000, www.tulsaworld.com/news/article.aspx?no=subj&articleid=L03
0900003&archive=yes (accessed February 10, 2009).

p. 99, Ibid.

p. 99, Ibid.

BOOKS

Dell, Pamela. *Wilma Mankiller: Chief of the Cherokee Nation.* Minneapolis: Compass Point Books, 2006.

Mankiller, Wilma. *Every Day Is a Good Day: Reflections of Contemporary Indigenous Women.* Golden, CO: Fulcrum Publishing, 2004.

Perdue, Theda. *The Cherokees.* New York: Chelsea House, 2004.

Sonneborn, Liz. *A to Z of American Indian Women*, Rev. ed. New York: Facts On File, 2007.

WEBSITES

Cherokee Nation
The official website of the Cherokee Nation of Oklahoma offers current information about the tribe as well as material about its history and culture.
www.cherokee.org

Eastern Band of Cherokee Indians
Created by the Eastern Band of Cherokee Indians, this site provides news from the tribe's reservation in North Carolina.
www.nc-cherokee.com

Cherokee Heritage Center
The mission of this historical society and museum, operated by the Cherokee Nation, is to "preserve, promote, and teach Cherokee History and Culture."
www.cherokeeheritage.org/index.html

BIBLIOGRAPHY

Edmunds, R. David, ed. *The New Warriors*. Lincoln: University of Nebraska Press, 2001.

Janda, Sarah Eppler. *Beloved Women: The Political Lives of LaDonna Harris and Wilma Mankiller*. DeKalb: Northern Illinois University Press, 2007.

Johnson, Troy R., ed. *You Are on Indian Land: Alcatraz Island, 1969–1971*. Los Angeles: American Indian Studies Center, 1995.

Mankiller, Wilma. *Every Day Is a Good Day: Reflections of Contemporary Indigenous Women*. Golden, CO: Fulcrum Publishing, 2004.

Mankiller, Wilma, and Michael Wallis. *Mankiller: A Chief and Her People*. New York: St. Martin's Press, 1993.

Marshall, Brenda Devore, and Molly A. Mayhead, eds. *Telling Political Lives: The Rhetorical Autobiographies of Women Leaders in the United States*. Lanham, MD: Lexington Books, 2008.

Nelson, Andrew. "Wilma Mankiller." *Salon*. November 20, 2001. www.salon.com/people/bc/2001/11/20/mankiller

Perdue, Theda. *Cherokee Women: Gender and Culture Change, 1700–1835*. Lincoln: University of Nebraska Press, 1998.

Sturtevant, William C., ed. *Handbook of North American Indians: Vol. 15, Southeast*. Washington, D.C.: Smithsonian Institution, 2004.

Taylor, Carolyn Anne et al, eds. *Voices from the Heartland*. Norman: University of Oklahoma Press, 2007.

INDEX

ABOUT THE AUTHOR

LIZ SONNEBORN is a freelance writer who has long lived in Brooklyn, New York. A graduate of Swarthmore College, she is the author of more than seventy books for children and adults. Sonneborn has written extensively about the history and culture of American Indian peoples, including children's books about the Apaches, Creeks, Shoshones, Chumash, Iroquois, Navajos, Cheyenne, Seminoles, and Choctaws. She is also the author of *The American West: An Illustrated History*, *Chronology of American Indian History*, and *A to Z of American Indian Women*.